The American
Buffalo
in
Transition

The flower-fed buffaloes of the spring
In the days of long ago,
Ranged where the locomotives sing
And the prairie flowers lie low.

The Flower-Fed Buffaloes
Vachel Lindsay, (1879-1931)

THE AMERICAN BUFFALO IN TRANSITION:

A HISTORICAL AND ECONOMIC SURVEY
OF THE
BISON
IN
AMERICA

by

J. Albert Rorabacher

NORTH STAR PRESS

Saint Cloud,   Minnesota

This book is typeset in 10 point Palatino roman type with Palatino display heads. The typesetting and printing was completed by Sentinel Printing Company, St. Cloud, Minnesota. The binding was crafted by Midwest Editions, Inc., Minneapolis, Minnesota. All maps, charts and graphs are by the author.

NORTH STAR PRESS
Post Office Box 451
St. Cloud, Minnesota 56301

Printed in the United States of America

Dedication

To Darius,

his very existence has been inspiration to me

PREFACE

The story of the transition of the American buffalo is a highly complex one. As civilization spread across the North American continent, the range and number of wild buffalo rapidly decreased. Unknowingly, the American people permitted the near extermination of the bison. Between 1800 and the 1890's, free-roaming buffalo in North America were reduced from an estimated 60 million to fewer than 20 wild bison in the United States.

Slowly the American people were awakened to the realization that the buffalo was near extinction. Through active work on the part of dedicated individuals, representatives in the Congress and White House, the Departments of Agriculture and the Interior, the buffalo was saved from extermination. Since that time the bison population in the United States has experienced a slow, but definite growth. Today, in excess of 17,000 bison exist under varying degrees of supervision ranging from private herds to restrictive zoos to large parks where the animals can again roam freely.

This book is an attempt to present a survey of the decimation of the bison; to consider the major factors that have influenced the growth in the United States's buffalo population since circa 1900. This book will further assess the historical and contemporary importance of these factors, and give a perspective to each factor insofar as it interrelates with the others and will further stimulate the steady growth of the American bison population.

The literature concerning the historical aspects of the buffalo is often highly contradictory, inaccurate, and generally lacking in objectivity. Authors have tended to rely ostensibly on the few *classics* in bison history without adequately acquainting their readers with the sources of their pronouncements. In addition, many scholars have accepted and perpetuated dogmatisms that were generated by early frontiersmen's tales and generalizations, and often these are irreconcilable with empirical fact. Consequently, it was incumbent upon me to collect more relevant and reliable data. Thus, a portion of this book comes from selective research, the use of questionnaires, personal correspondence, and field work.

Selective research was undertaken to compile a vast bibliography concerning the bison. The selection of materials for inclusion in this book was difficult. Well over 900 separate titles were collected. Then came the culling from all of these and the selection of materials that are accurate, uncompromising, and above all not incumbered with sentimentality. The bibliography at the end of the book and the References and Further Readings at the end of most chapters provide the reader with the most representative works of the original 900 titles.

Questionnaires were sent to randomly-selected bison raisers throughout the United States. The questionnaires sought general information concerning factors that have influenced the increase of the bison population since circa 1900 and reasons for the possible continuation of this increase.

Detailed, empirical information was collected through personal correspondence with selected bison raisers and others known to be interested in, or knowledgeable of, bison. These persons were queried about specific matters related to the major factors influencing the increase in the bison population.

Field work was conducted which entailed an extensive journey through the West. The original journey was undertaken in the summer of 1968, but each summer since has added to the collection of data. During these trips, it was my intent to personally contact as many agencies and individuals who owned herds of buffalo in the United States as was practical. This field work resulted in a wealth of data heretofore unrecorded concerning the bison.

In the course of writing this book, I received the advice, encouragement, and assistance from many people. To mention each person would, in itself, necessitate the addition of many pages. However, I must give special thanks to Dr. Frederick J. Simoons of the University of California at Davis, who unknowingly is largely responsible for the very existence of this book; Dr. Michael E. Sabbagh of the University of Texas; the National Buffalo Association, and especially Dr. Dwain W. Cummings; my mother (who because of an untimely and premature death was never able to read this work) and father; my grandparents; Dr. Harry C. Cliadakis of the University of Wisconsin-Green Bay; and last, but far from least, to my wife Wisty, who helped compile data, criticized my writing, argued with me, and spent many hours toiling over the manuscript. To all of these people and those who remained unmentioned, thank you for everything.

J. Albert Rorabacher
Green Bay, Wisconsin
June 1971

TABLE OF CONTENTS

The American
Buffalo
in
Transition

The first known drawing of the American bison. This picture was printed in Gomara's *Historia de los Indios Saragossa*, published in 1552-1553.

Chapter One

The Buffalo, an Introduction

When the Spanish conquistadores first penetrated North America in the sixteenth century, they encountered a novel, hump-backed mammal of great stature and strength. They called the previously unrecorded animal "cattle or Cibola," or "kine." In the seventeenth century, French *voyageurs* exploring the North American plains referred to the same animals as *les boeufs*, meaning oxen or beeves. The later arriving English found it difficult to pronounce *les boeufs*, and thus changed the name to "la buff." The name of this unique animal became increasingly distorted, being called at various times "buffle," "buffler," "buffillo," and ultimately "buffalo." The first person known to officially use the term buffalo was Thomas Salmon in his 1749 work entitled: *A New Geographical and Historical Grammar.*

Scientifically, the term buffalo is incorrect when referring to the large, hump-backed mammal of North America. True buffalo are indigenous only to Africa and Asia, and belong to the genus *Bubalus*. The proper Latin name of the American buffalo is *Bison bison;* however, common usage has made buffalo an acceptable synonym for the American bison.

In historical accounts, reference is made to three varieties of American buffalo—the Wood, Mountain, and Plains types.

The Wood buffalo ranged in the foothills of the Rockies of the United States and in the forests of Canada near Lake Athabaska. The Mountain buffalo ranged in the Rocky Mountains of both the United States and Canada; and the Plains-type ranged widely on the plains of the United States and Canada. For all intents and purposes, the Wood and Mountain buffalo are the same species, and differ only slightly from the Plains buffalo.

The Wood buffalo (including the so-called Mountain-type) looks very much like the buffalo of the plains. However, the Wood buffalo is somewhat smaller, its legs are shorter and stronger, and its pelage is considerably darker than that of the Plains buffalo. These differences have caused the Wood buffalo to be given a sub-specific classification under the scientific name *Bison bison Athabascae Rhoads*.

Many scientists believe that no distinction should be made between the Plains and Wood buffalo. Such scientists feel that the observable differences between the two varieties of buffalo are merely responses to different physical environments. That is, Wood buffalo are smaller and shorter legged because the forests or mountains in which they live are not conducive to large animals. Further, the food which Wood buffalo rely upon is much different from that of the Plains buffalo. According to some early writers, Wood buffalo shun the grasses of the plains in preference to the graze found in the woods of the Rockies. The belief in the likeness of the Plains and Wood buffalo is supported by evolutionary trends displayed by the buffalo of Yellowstone National Park. The park buffalo are descendants of Plains buffalo. In less than one hundred years, the size and color of the buffalo have changed, presumably in response to the mountainous terrain of the park and the available food. Overall the Yellowstone buffalo have become smaller and their coats darker. Today, the park zoologist considers the animals to be Wood buffalo because of this changed appearance. Thus, it is doubtful that the differences between the

Wood and Plains buffalo are significant enough to consider the animals as separate species.

The origin of the buffalo in North America is not completely clear, nor is the archeological information clear upon which the final conclusions of origin are based. At one time, it was hypothesized that the Plains-type buffalo was the parent stock of all American buffalo types. However, this belief has been discredited, for archeological findings indicate that the buffalo had its origin elsewhere.

There remain two very similar hypotheses of the buffalo's origin. Both theories agree on the origin of the parent stock, but differ in the direction of the evolutionary process required to create the American buffalo. The first hypothesis was proposed in 1886 by Ernest Thompson Seton. It supposes that the American buffalo descended from an Eurasiatic form of buffalo, through the Woodlands type, to the Plains type. Based on recent archeological findings, this hypothesis seems to be the most probable; however, the second theory has not been entirely disproven.

The second hypothesis suggest a direct descent from an Eurasiatic ancestor to the Plains buffalo, followed by the development of the Woodland variety. This hypothesis requires two evolutionary processes—the creation of the Plains type from the Eurasiatic parent stock, followed by the creation of the Wood type which is most like the original Eurasiatic ancestor. Although there might have been sufficient time for these two processes to have taken place, it is highly improbable that natural selection would have resulted in such back-stepping in the evolutionary process.

In either case, it is suggested that the American buffalo ultimately evolved from an Eurasiatic ancestor. Some authorities believe the American buffalo descended directly from the Lithuanian variety—the Wisent or Zuhr; others, like Yermoloff, believe the American buffalo descended from the Wisent of the Caucasus Mountains. Still others contend that the buffalo came from a hybrid of the Lithuanian Wisent and Caucasus types. No matter what the actual parent stock, both theories depend on the existence of a Bering land bridge between Asia and North America. After the Bering land bridge disappeared, the migrating buffalo were isolated from their ancestors, and eventually produced our American buffalo types.

Dr. Lutz Heck, Berlin

The Wisent (*Bison Bonasus*).

In stature the American buffalo is the largest game animal in North America. A full grown bull stands approximately six feet high at the shoulder, is roughly nine feet long, and weighs between 2,000 and 2,600 pounds.[1] There have been records of bulls weighing up to 3,000 and 3,500 pounds; however, these latter weights are undoubtedly exaggerated. Cows are generally smaller, weighing between 1,300 and 1,500 pounds.

[1] Much of the information describing the buffalo has been adapted from Martin S. Garretson's 1938 book entitled: *The American Bison*, New York, New York Zoological Society.

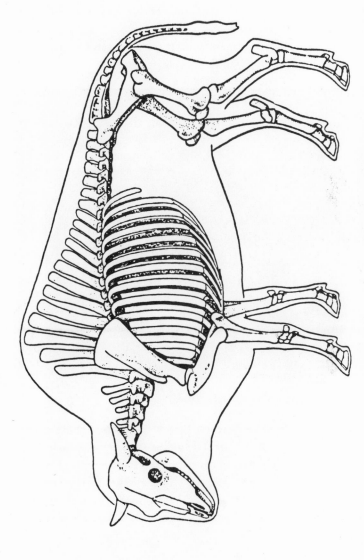

Skeleton structure of the American bison showing the distinctive dorsal vertebrae, or bearing structure for the "hump."

The American Bison (Bison Bison Americanus). This animal is a typical example of the Plain buffalo bull.

The most outstanding feature of the buffalo is its massive head and forequarters, which seem somewhat out of proportion to the hindquarters. The so-called "hump" gives the buffalo its distinctive appearance. The hump is formed by a gradual elongation of the dorsal vertebrae, beginning just ahead of the hips and reaching its maximum height just above the front shoulder. From this point, the hump drops almost straight down to the neck. The extended vertebrae support a large layer of choice, tender meat.

Buffalo meat is very much like that of common cattle. With the extension of the dorsal vertebrae, buffalo provide more meat from the same region than do common cattle. Meat from the hump of buffalo cows is generally more tender and sweeter than that from bulls. It is often difficult to distinguish between a similar cut of meat from buffalo and cattle. In general, buffalo meat is a little more dark red in color than beef and does not have as much marbling (streaks of fat running through the meat). In flavor, again the two meats are very similar. As a consequence of these characteristics, early North American settlers and hunters readily used buffalo meat as a substitute for their common fare of beef, for the early beef cattle were tough and lacked the flavor which we expect in beef today.

In late fall or early winter the buffalo's coat is a rich, dark brown in color and is of high quality. As winter progresses the coat changes color, becoming much paler by spring. Simultaneously the coat begins to loosen and hang in patches, until the coat is completely shed in late spring. The buffalo rubs against almost any available object, or will roll in the dirt, to hasten the shedding. The rolling may also satisfy the animal's need to scratch, for as new hair comes in, it causes an uncomfortable itching. For a very short period buffalo appear to be almost completely void of hair except around the head, hump and fore-legs. By fall the buffalo are again protected with a new brown coat.

The normal "family" grouping of the buffalo during the Spring—massive bull on guard, cow resting and tending the new calf.

Guardians of the herd. The massive bulls shoulder to shoulder protecting the cows and young from wolves.

White, or albino, buffalo represent the greatest contrast to the normal brown color. Albinism among all animals is occasionally encountered and is to be expected genetically. However, among buffalo this phenomenon seems to be disproportionately low. When millions of buffalo roamed the Great Plains, very few albinos were ever seen. Early writers, who did encounter white buffalo, attempted to explain the existence of the animals by stating that they were hybrids of common cattle and light-colored buffalo.[2] This explanation is somewhat dubious as will be seen in light of information given in Chapter 6. Other writers mention white buffalo, but as Frank G. Roe points out, these were usually only partially white, pied or spotted animals, and not true albinos. In modern times there has been only one account of a pure white, mature buffalo. In 1933 a white buffalo bull, named Big Medicine, was born on the National Bison Range in Montana. The animal lived on that range for twenty-six years. When Big Medicine died in 1959, his hide was taken to the Montana Historical Society Museum, in Helena, where it was mounted for public display. There are other accounts of white buffalo being born, two in Alaska, but none of these lived to maturity.

Between July and October each year the general level of activity within buffalo herds increases, for this is the "running" or mating season. After a gestation period of approximately nine months, the cows produce a yellowish-red calf. Much like a newborn domestic calf, a buffalo calf is able to follow its mother soon after birth. The cows suckle their calves until the following spring when the yearlings are displaced by newborn calves. Only rarely do buffalo cows produce twins.

As a buffalo calf grows older, its coat darkens. By its first autumn the calf is nearly the same color as its parents. By the second month of life the calf shows signs of a hump. At approximately six months, horns begin to appear as straight

---

[2] For an extensive account of the "white buffalo," see F. G. Roe's work: *White Buffalo*, Ottawa, Royal Society of Canada, 1944.

spikes. By the time the young buffalo is able to breed, at two or three years of age, the horns begin to curve upward. By five or six years of age, the buffalo reaches its full growth, and the horns form semi-circular curves. From maturity until death, a life span of approximately 20 to 30 years, the buffalo's horns add many growth rings and become very thick at the base.

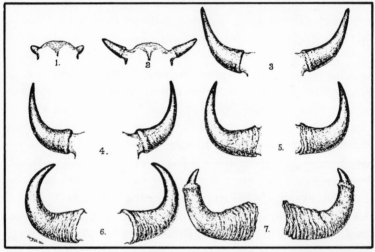

Hornaday

Development of the Horns of the American Bison. 1. The Calf. 2. The Yearling. 3. Spike Bull, 2 years old. 4. Spike Bull, 3 years old. 5. Bull, 4 years old. 6. Bull, 11 years old. 7. Old "stub-horn" Bull, 20 years old.

Normally buffalo are rather lazy, mild-dispositioned and inoffensive creatures. This description is not, however, always the case, for buffalo are highly unpredictable. Even when a buffalo is hand-raised from a calf, it can *never* be trusted nor relied upon. There are many accounts of people becoming overly confident and careless when around buffalo and being either injured or killed by a charging animal. One such account, given by Martin Garretson, tells of Dick Rock who owned a buffalo bull which Rock had raised from a calf. The animal had become so tame that it would allow Rock to ride upon it around the corral. One day, after Rock had finished riding

the "pet" buffalo and was walking away, the animal charged
and gored Rock to death.

J. Dwyer

A strong young bull showing the shedding of his pelage in Spring.

Buffalo are grazing animals, dependent on grasses for the
bulk of their diet. Unlike the Plains type, the Wood buffalo
was a browser and subsisted on the substantial areas of vegeta-
tion available for browsing in the foothills of the Rockies and
in the forests of the eastern United States. The plains of the
United States and Canada provided millions of acres of many
different grasses upon which the Plains buffalo subsisted. The
most important grass was buffalo, grama, or mesquite grass.
By nature grama is a very short grass, roughly two to three
inches high, and usually found in small bunches. Because of
its hardy nature, this grass was ideally suited to the Great Plains
where rainfall is often very unreliable. Where water was available in greater quantities, as in river valleys, the buffalo grass
grew to be a foot high in uninterrupted masses. There were
other grasses, such as wild oats, beard grass, purple bunch
grass, blue grass, blue stem, that the buffalo utilized when
grama was not available. When, because of drought or grass
fires on the plains, buffalo were forced to search for non-grass

foods, they would browse on some species of sage brush, but they would never eat the so-called "loco weed." Buffalo seemed to sense that loco weed produced a sort of madness in animals. This is one quality that horses and domestic cattle do not share for these beasts will often eat loco weed and become demented.

Range of the Buffalo

The American buffalo was once the most widely distributed mammal in the world—with the exception of man. As Europeans began settling the eastern coast of the North American continent in the early seventeenth century, free-roaming bison were slowly extending their range in every direction from the central plains. In the West the buffalo herds were pushing through the Sierra Nevadas toward the Pacific coast. In the East they had crossed the Mississippi River and penetrated the Appalachians almost to the Atlantic. At its fartherest limits, the buffalo range extended from central Florida in the Southeast; to the southern region of modern Coahuila and Durango states in Mexico in the Southwest; to the eastern shore of Lake Erie in the Northeast, and to the area immediately north of Great Slave Lake in the Northwest. In the East, the range extended almost to the Atlantic seaboard and, in the West, to the valleys of the Snake and Columbia Rivers, and into the foothills of the Blue Mountains of southern Oregon and northern California. Within this greatly varied range, a range composed of mountains, forests, and prairie, an estimated sixty to one hundred and fifty million bison dwelled.[3] See Map I.

[3] The precise number of buffalo that existed at any one time will always remain purely conjectural. The estimates vary greatly from writer to writer. Some estimates are as high as 150 to 200 million buffalo; others are as low as 50 million. Although the estimates vary greatly, the most oft quoted figure is 60 million buffalo. Therefore, all figures used in this book will be based on the assumption that there were 60 million buffalo—a figure computed long after the buffalo had been almost exterminated from the territories of the United States, and one that might well be entirely too low.

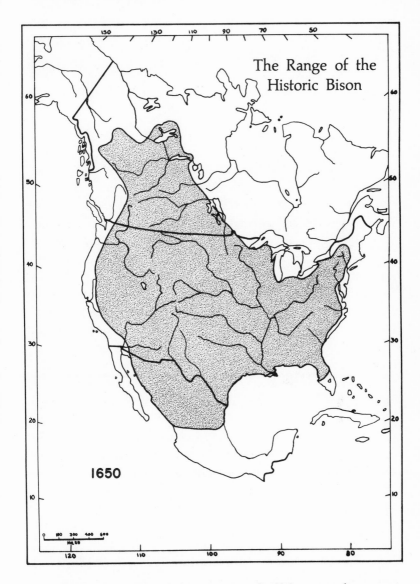

The Range of the
Historic Bison

1650

Today the range of the American buffalo is much greater than in any earlier period, although the numbers of buffalo are significantly fewer than in the seventeenth century. While

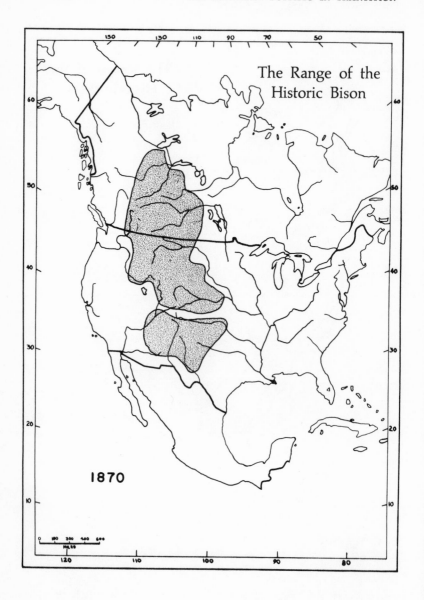

The Range of the Historic Bison

1870

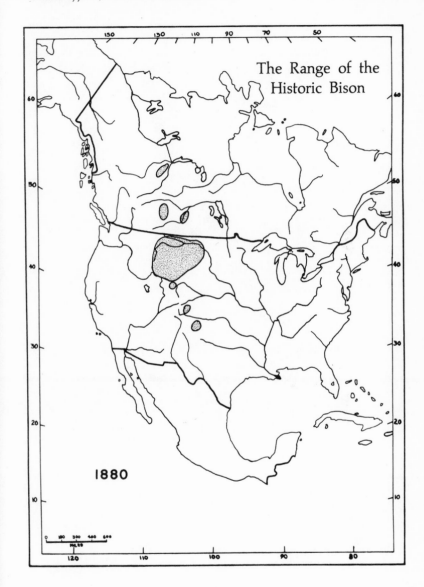

The Range of the
Historic Bison

1880

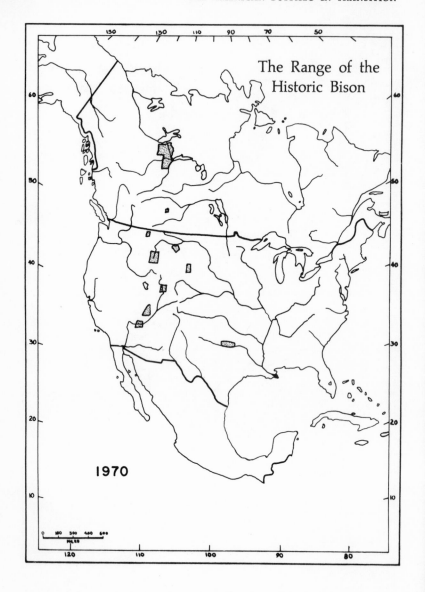

The Range of the
Historic Bison

1970

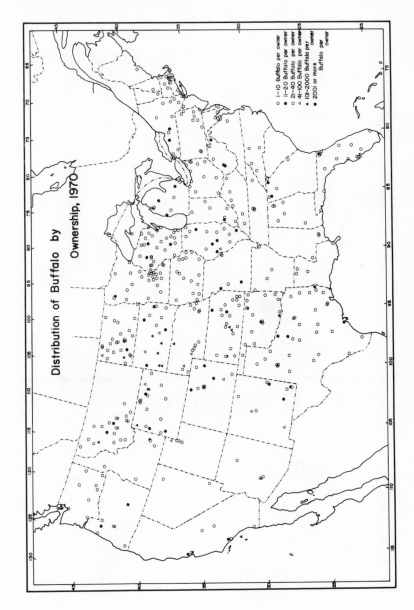

Distribution of Buffalo by Ownership, 1970

o 1-10 Buffalo per owner
• 11-20 Buffalo per owner
□ 21-40 Buffalo per owner
△ 41-100 Buffalo per owner
▲ 101-2000 Buffalo per owner
■ 2001 or more Buffalo per owner

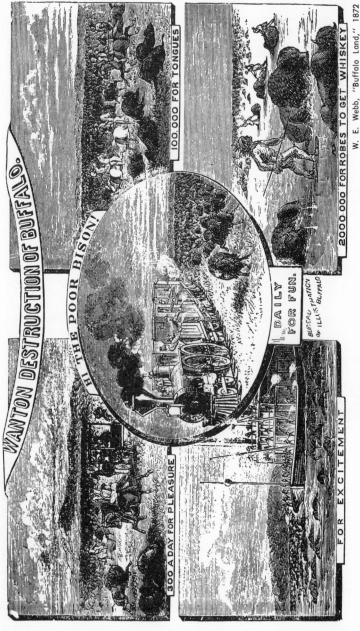

WANTON DESTRUCTION OF BUFFALO.

HI THE POOR BISON!

100,000 FOR TONGUES

2,000,000 FOR ROBES TO GET WHISKEY

DAILY FOR FUN.

BUFFALO EXTIRPATION OF ILLUS BUFFALO

300 A DAY FOR PLEASURE

FOR EXCITEMENT

W. E. Webb, "Buffalo Land," 1872

Protest against extermination of the buffalo began in the 'seventies.

18

the buffalo population of the United States alone is estimated to be from 15,000 to 30,000 head, their range now encompasses nearly every state of the Union, including Hawaii. In addition, in Canada buffalo are found in nearly every province. As a consequence of man's interest in the buffalo, man has increased the range of the buffalo and increased the number of entirely new habitats within which the buffalo is now capable of surviving. Thus, with the aid of man, the buffalo may well be one of those rare animals with the capacity to survive well in numerous and highly different physical habitats, from semitropical Florida to the mountains of Alaska, and the drier portions of the American southwest (See Modern Distribution Map).

Until the nineteenth century man had little effect on the habits of the buffalo, although the Indian had been killing buffalo since Ice Age times. Later Indians and explorer-fur trappers killed only small numbers of buffalo for food and raw materials. Only on occasion would the Indians kill more buffalo than they immediately needed, and this was usually done only when the Indians wished to trade with other tribes or with the white traders. However, the natural balance was sharply disrupted as the white man's civilization began extending into the heart of the buffalo's domain—the Great Plains. Besides the white man's careless use and misuse of the buffalo, the Indian's attitude toward the buffalo changed, and soon many Indians joined in killing buffalo for a previously unheard of reason—profit.

References and Further Readings[4]

Allen, J. A. "The American Bisons, Living and Extinct," *Memoirs of the Geological Survey of Kentucky,* Vol. 1, Part 2, 1876, pp. i-236.

[4] The References and Further Readings located at the end of each chapter are provided for the reader's interest. They are in no way intended to be complete, nor are they more than representative of the great many works written on the buffalo.

Bartram, Wm. "Travels in Georgia and Florida in 1773-74," *Transactions of the American Philosophical Society*, Vol. 33(2), 1943, pp. 117-242.

Garretson, M. S. *The American Bison*, New York: New York Zoological Society, 1938.

Hornaday, Wm. T. "The Extermination of the American Bison," *Smithsonian Annual Report for 1887*, Part 2, 1889, pp. 367-548.

Merriam, C. H. "Early Records of Buffalo in 'California' (Nevada, Utah, and Southwestern Wyoming)," *Journal of Mammalogy*, Vol. 45(4), 1922, pp. 54-55.

Roe, F. G. *The North American Buffalo*, Toronto: University of Toronto Press, 1970.

Rostlund, E. "The Geographic Range of the Historic Bison in the Southeast," *Annals of the AAG*, 50(4), 1960, pp. 395-407.

Dover "Pictorial Archive"

An early drawing of the bison from *The Figures of Bewick's Quadrupeds*, 2nd ed. published in Newcastle, England in 1824.

Chapter Two

The Decimation of the American Bison

The near extermination of the bison in the United States was almost an unavoidable chapter in American history. Today factual information on this unprecedented slaughter of wild animals has been obscured by time and romantic folklore. Nevertheless, a close and critical investigation of relatively recent American history and attitudes reveals three primary reasons for the killing of approximately 60 million bison.

The most important reason for the bison's decimation was the development of our American civilization. A growing eastern population caused many people to seek new crop or grazing land in the less-restricting expanses of the untamed West. Frequently the great number of free-roaming buffalo represented an obstacle to the utilization of the western lands. Consequently, frontiersmen felt justified in killing large numbers of the bothersome and often destructive buffalo.

The explosive initiative of nineteenth century Americans also influenced the killing of bison. This initiative was not destructive until two factors helped turn initiative into greed. On one hand, the exaggerated reports sent east to prospective settlers encouraged the belief that the West held potential riches for anyone hardy enough to find and exploit them. The second factor was the apparent abundance of buffalo in the

West. Buffalo seemed to be everywhere and in unending numbers. This tended to inhibit any self-imposed restrictions on the number of bison killed by a single individual. One factor complimented the other; and as long as an economic profit could be gained by selling either buffalo meat, robes, or hides, the buffalo were tracked down and killed.

The third reason for the buffalo's destruction was a combination of the animal's physical characteristics and its nature. Buffalo have very poor eyesight. Only when a man ventures extremely close to a buffalo can the man be detected. Further, by nature buffalo are lazy and not easily moved. Using these characteristics to their advantage, Indians would cover themselves with wolf skins and sneak up on buffalo to within bow-and-arrow killing range. Later, professional hunters often used a technique known as "the stand," whereby a hunter would partially conceal himself down-wind of a herd and shoot directly into the herd. The buffalo would seldom scatter even after hearing the crack of a rifle or seeing wounded members of the herd fall. The naturally gregarious buffalo often formed great herds numbering into the millions. With such a massive grouping of animals, it was not uncommon for a single stand to result in the killing of a hundred or more bison.

The Public Archives of Canada

A Surround. An early painting by A. J. Miller, showing the plains Indians on the group hunt cutting the game from the massive main herd.

A Paul Kane painting showing Indians driving buffalo into a log corral or compound for killing.

Hunt painting by John Mix Stanley (1845) which illustrates the use by Plains Indians of the horse and lance for close in hunting and killing of buffalo.

A highly romantic painting by George Catlin showing the Indians on the hunt. The scene, which belies Catlin's usual honesty in illustration, presents a very improbable event, or some very incompetent Indian hunters.

An early colored lithograph signed "A. H." which illustrates the short, stout bow used by the horse Indians for the running hunt.

Peabody Museum, Harvard Univ.

The buffalo attempting to flee from the snowshoed Indian hunters break through the crusted snow and become easy victims. From a watercolor painting by Peter Rindisbacher.

Coe Collection, Yale Univ.

A Paul Kane painting which shows a mixed group of Indians and troopers on the buffalo hunt. All of these paintings show the hazard of riding among the running buffalo during the hunt.

East of the Mississippi River

The number of bison east of the Mississippi River was never very large although, in many historical accounts, authors mention the presence of hundreds, even thousands of buffalo especially around the salt licks and hot springs of Kentucky, Virginia, and Pennsylvania. Two theories attempt to explain the presence of bison east of the Mississippi. The first holds that, because of population pressures on the Great Plains, some buffalo forded the Mississippi River early in the sixteenth century and became permanent inhabitants of the eastern United States. The second theory proposes that, because of local pasturage deficiencies and drought conditions in the West, buffalo periodically crossed the Mississippi in search of food. After a time these buffalo annually migrated into the East, some eventually finding their way beyond the salt licks of Kentucky and Virginia to within a few miles of the Atlantic seacoast. In either case, by the eighteenth century the buffalo had become a relatively common animal west of the Appalachians and, occasionally, east of those mountains.

Explorers and early frontiersmen frequently crossed the Appalachians into Kentucky by way of so-called "buffalo roads." These paths were created by herds of buffalo forced to travel in narrow routes to and from salt licks. Later joined by settlers, the adventurers obtained much of their food supply from buffalo. Many settlers initially found it easier to hunt buffalo, elk, or deer than to clear the forests and begin farming. In fact, some early writers suggest that the real beginnings of agriculture in this area were hindered until the bison became scarce.[1]

Among the Kentucky settlers who were actively farming, their small herds of domestic stock were far too valuable to be slaughtered for food or leather. The buffalo, on the other

[1] See Fortescue Cuming's "Sketches of a Tour in the Western Country," in R. G. Thwaites, *Early Western Travels*, Vol. 4, for his observations concerning the retardation of agriculture because of the "easy life" by the gun.

hand, could, and did, serve in place of domestic stock in this regard. Growing cattle herds might have aided in the demise of the buffalo by competing with buffalo for food, and by destroying the cane breaks which were the common hiding place for buffalo. Thus, with their graze gone, their hiding place destroyed, and their value as a food animal realized, the buffalo was the first large game animal to be hunted and killed-off in the eastern United States.

The disappearance of the buffalo from the lands east of the Mississippi River was a slow and gradual process. As the American population expanded and people pressed into hitherto unused lands, sanctuaries of the buffalo became fewer and fewer, as did the number of bison. The eastern bison were never needlessly slaughtered as buffalo later were in the West. Rather, the demise of the buffalo in the East resulted from too many settler/hunters in need of food and raw materials, and too few buffalo. Had the number of buffalo in the East been proportionately as large as the number in the West, the eastern buffalo might well have remained in existence until late in the nineteenth century. However, history records that the last free-roaming buffalo east of the Mississippi was killed in the early 1830's, and the majority were gone well before this.

West of the Mississippi River

West of the Mississippi River the nature of the buffalo slaughter was quite different. First there were always far more buffalo on the Great Plains than there were in the East which tended to encourage exploitation. Secondly, the buffalo of the West were seldom killed explicitly for their immediate food value as had been the case in the East. Rather, in the West the majority of bison were killed directly for economic gain. During the first half of the nineteenth century bison meat, especially the hump and tongue of cows, was the most valuable part of the animal. The robes taken from bison were either sold in England, or sold as blankets or decorations to people

Harper's Weekly

This 1874 woodcut romanticizes the taking of the buffalo hides. The skinner's corduroy suit was little use for the bloody, stinking work of a hide taker.

A Sharps Side-Hammer 45-90 caliber rifle. This heavy barreled gun weighes 16 pounds without ammunition! This rifle and its companion 50-70 models were the favorite of the money hunters.

Jim Goerger Gun Shop, Austin, Minn.

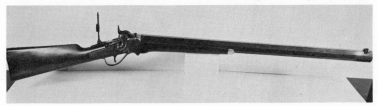

in the United States. By the second half of the nineteenth century, however, technological advancements in the United States made it far more profitable to kill bison for their hides; this was the time of the most intense and wasteful killing of bison in North America.

In 1803 the United States purchased the Louisiana Territory from France—an expanse of land that contained most of the American Great Plains. The Lewis and Clark expedition was dispatched by President Jefferson to survey the new territory west of the Mississippi. After the findings of the expedition were reported to the public, thousands of adventurers traveled west by wagon or on foot, seeking free land and new opportunity beyond the Mississippi River. In the following three decades, these people established themselves as farmers, ranchers, hunters, and military personnel on the Great Plains. Each group, in its own way, contributed to the reduction of the buffalo population and range.

Until western farmers and ranchers were able to live on the products of their land, they valued the bison as a constant source of food. As such, only that number of buffalo needed to satisfy nutritional demands was killed. Once the farmers and ranchers became economically successful, however, wild, free-roaming buffalo were considered to be more destructive than valuable. Consequently, to protect their lands from being over-grazed, their crops from being eaten or trampled, and their livestock from being run off, many settlers killed buffalo without reservation.

Individual hunters also killed buffalo for food, but of greater importance to independent hunters was the commercial value of bison meat. Although there were relatively few professional hunters in the first half of the nineteenth century, their intense desire for economic gain led to the killing of tens of thousands of buffalo annually.

The report brought back by the Lewis and Clark expedition also wetted the appetites of fur traders, for the report recounted

Two skinners working the hide off of a monster bull during the season of 1882 on the Northern range.

Old picture caption on this reads, "5 minutes work on Buffalo cows."

A typical hunters dugout camp on the buffalo range. Note bighorn sheep
head over top of entryway. This place was called Camp Emmet during
the winter of 1882.

the abundance of wildlife to be found in the northwest. Soon
fur trading posts were established and professional hunting
groups hired. As early as 1820 the Red River Settlement, a
prosperous trading post on the Red River in Manitoba, Canada,
began sending out annual buffalo hunting expeditions. In the
first year alone the hunters filled over 500 carts with robes
of buffalo.[2]

Other firms followed the lead of the Red River Settlement.
The American Fur Company established trading posts along

[2] For a description of the Red River Settlement's development, see
Alexander Ross's *Red River Settlement* (1856, London: Smith, Elder, and
Co.); and Louis Wood's *The Red River Colony* (1920, Toronto: n.p.).

the Missouri River, at the mouth of the Teton and Yellowstone Rivers, and at many advantageous locations along other western rivers. By 1840 the American Fur Company posts had sent 67,000 robes to St. Louis; and in 1848, 110,000 robes and 25,000 tongues were sent to St. Louis. Most of the shipments from the valley of the Missouri were sent via river boat because it was impossible to use pack animals to transport such large quantities of robes and tongues. The Hudson's Bay Company of Canada also engaged in the buffalo robe trade; however, because of its remote northern position, the Hudson's Bay Company was much less influential in the robe trade than the American Fur Company.

As the Red River Settlement expanded its fur-trading operation, it simultaneously reduced the number of buffalo in the immediate area. So efficient were the Red River hunters that they annually brought in over 500,000 robes. In addition, settlers and other independent hunters in the area killed large numbers of buffalo, again for their robes, and only occasionally for their meat. By 1847 nearly all the buffalo had been killed in the area of the northeastern Dakota Territory, northern Minnesota, Manitoba, and parts of Saskatchewan. Thus, it was no longer economically feasible for the Red River Settlement to send out buffalo hunting parties, for the distance hunters had to travel, and the area they had to cover to find sufficient quantities of buffalo were too great. Not long after 1850 the settlement was deserted but for a few merchants who served the local settlers.

During the later years of the Red River Settlement, the hunters were forced to exploit the lands of the Plains Cree Indians. Initially, neither the white hunters nor the Indians unduly disrupted or disturbed one another's activities. However, as buffalo became increasingly scarce, the Cree became extremely protective of their traditional hunting grounds. Eventually the Cree forbade all white buffalo hunters to enter or pass through the Cree lands, thereby straining Indian-white relations.

Indian hunter invoking the Buffalo Spirit to return to the hunting grounds.

After the lands of the Cree had been over-hunted, a similar situation occurred in the traditional hunting lands of the Sioux, Pawnees, Omahas, Ponca, Yankton, Santee, and several other Indian tribes (including the southern portion of the Dakota Territory, southwestern Minnesota, and northern Nebraska). Items offered in trade by white hunters induced many of these tribes to join in killing large numbers of buffalo exclusively for the animals' robes. Once again, so effective were the Indian and white hunters that by 1870 the buffalo were almost entirely eliminated from this north central region; and by 1880 the last buffalo in the region was killed by an Indian hunter. The loss was particularly great to the Indians who had aided in the destruction of their major source of food in exchange for a few blankets, guns, ammunition, whiskey, and other "civilized" supplies. Emotionally the Indians could not accept the fact that they had helped the white man destroy the buffalo, nor that they themselves had completed the extermination. Consequently, the Indians blamed white men in general for the extermination of buffalo on Indian lands. This hostile attitude endangered the lives of all whites living in the area.

The first United States military posts in the West were established to promote civil order among the settlers and hunters, and to provide them with protection against occasional attacks by "savage" Indians. In the beginning, the military, too, was interested in buffalo primarily as a source of nutrition. However, by the middle of the nineteenth century when the accumulative killing of buffalo had become a virtual slaughter, the animal-land balance of the Great Plains was upset and the life-style of the Plains Indians seriously threatened. This further provoked the already antagonized Indians and ultimately resulted in the Indian Wars. Some perceptive military officials became concerned about the killing of buffalo as it affected the overall balance of peace and life in the West. However, other than the few military officials who attempted to halt, or at least control the killing in the interest of either conservation or peace with the Indians, most government officials did not interfere with the slaughter of buffalo on the Great Plains.[3]

During the several decades beyond the mid-nineteenth century, the bison slaughter in the western United States became increasingly intense and complicated, primarily as a result of two technological advancements—the completion of a network of railroads connecting the eastern United States with the developing West; and the discovery of a tanning process for converting bison hides into commercially valuable leather.[4] The influence of the railroads on the bison population and range was both direct and indirect.

The most obvious direct result of the railroad construction was the killing of bison to feed railroad workmen, as well as to occasionally clear a path through bison herds for rails to be laid. Because of this unsettling and wanton killing of bison, within a short time after the completion of the Union Pacific railroad in the early 1860's, there was a path of at least 25 miles on either side of the railway void of buffalo. The once almost continuous herd of approximately 60 million bison on the Great Plains thus became clearly divided into a distinct Southern and Northern herd. The Southern herd is estimated to have included over 20 million bison, centered around the area of what was to become Garden City, Kansas. The Northern herd was considerably larger with an estimated population of 40 million bison. It stretched across the northern Great Plains, north of the Platte River, to as far north as the Great Slave Lake, and from the eastern portions of the Dakota Territory

[3] See Chapter 3 for a more detailed discussion of some of the military personnel's attitudes toward the buffalo and the Indians; also the attitude of many people in high-appointed or elective offices in the United States government.

[4] Entire books have been written about the extermination of the buffalo. Any attempt to survey the period of extermination can only hope to give the reader a glimpse of what was occurring. There were many events and influences that happened simultaneously; however, for the sake of organization and clarity, they will be treated as almost unrelated happenings although they were often closely related.

almost to the Pacific coast. The largest part of the Northern herd roamed the North Central plains of the United States and into the Rocky Mountain foothills of Canada.

By contributing to the population and economic growth of the western society, the railroads served as a catalyst in the further reduction of the bison population and range. Men and women, who earlier would not risk the dangers of traveling to, and living in, the West, looked upon the increasingly reliable railroads as a kind of security linking the "wild West" with the protection of the more familiar East. Consequently, when the Union Pacific railroad was completed, the number of people willing and anxious to travel west greatly increased. New farms and ranches were established, followed by the growth of communities and towns, followed by still more farms and ranches. As had happened earlier, these settlers killed nearby bison to protect their crops, domestic herds, and their communities. Then, too, widespread tales of western riches continued to lure adventurers, who wanted to "get rich quick," in even greater numbers than before. Finally, many former railroad construction workers, left stranded on the plains when their work was done, remained to start a new life in the recently opened land. Not all of these hopeful people were able to make their earlier dreams become a reality. Because of the proximity of the large bison herds, many of the disillusioned adventurers joined the increasing number of professional hunters in killing bison to provide for their livelihood.

The improved iron avenues of commerce and communication did, indeed, provide a stronger link between the East and West. Because trade was so greatly facilitated, new eastern markets were established to sell western products, among them bison robes and meat, and especially the tongue which was considered to be a delicacy. The use of bison robes was still limited to blankets and ornaments. However, as the demand for bison meat increased, so did the number of professional hunters on the Great Plains.

J. H. Moser

This painting by J. H. Moser shows how the stand hunter worked from a hidden ridge down wind from the herd. His side hammer Sharps would grow hot from the steady firing of cartridges from his near-at-hand ammunition belt.

A scene at Rath and Wrights' Buffalo Hide Yard in 1878. The picture shows some 40,000 buffalo hides being readied for shipment from Dodge City, Kansas.

Denver Public Library

In 1869, John W. Mooar, a professional meat hunter, sent several buffalo hides to his brother in the hope that the hides could be sold. Mooar's brother was unable to sell the hides. Eventually he gave them to a Pennsylvania tannery. In 1871 the tannery discovered a process for tanning buffalo hides into commercially valuable leather. Within a year new markets for hides developed in the East; and agents were immediately sent to major western towns to deal solely in buffalo hides. The relative value of bison products quickly changed. According to William T. Hornaday, with the discovery of the tanning process, the hide constituted nine-tenths of the buffalo's total value; the meat, hair, head, horns, etc., constituted the remaining one-tenth. Hides increased in value from virtually nothing to between one and three dollars apiece.

Requests for hides became so numerous that professional hunters collectively killed thousands of buffalo daily throughout the year. When meat had been the most valuable and desired product of the buffalo, hunters gave the buffalo a reprieve during the so-called "running season" when the animal's meat was unpalatable. However, varying qualities of valuable hides could be obtained year-round. The finest hides, which were made into coats, were ordinarily obtained in the late fall or early winter. Hides of lesser quality obtained during the fall and winter were made into blankets and other decorations. The poorest hides, which could be made into machinery belting, could be obtained during the remainder of the year. Preference was given to the killing of bison cows, for their hides were of higher quality and more easily worked than those of bulls, and, when desired, the meat from cows was far more tender. The year-round killing of bison cows drastically lessened the birth potential of the herds. Thus, it was almost impossible for the herds to replenish even a small portion of their reduced number.

So eager were professional hunters in acquiring hides that they were wasteful in their killing and use of buffalo. R. C. McCormick, Arizona representative to the House of Repre-

This woodcut by Berghaus shows the trainmen and passengers shooting buffalo from the train along the Kansas-Pacific Railroad. No animals were kept for meat.

sentatives in the early 1870's, told of a man who killed at least 99 animals in one day. From his days as a youth in Arizona, McCormick was convinced that no single group of hunters and skinners could make use of this many dead animals before some of the hides were spoiled by decomposition as the animals laid on the plains. Further, ninety-nine percent of all the available meat from the slaughtered buffalo was wasted as hide hunters either ignored the meat for the sake of expediency, or chose to strip the carcasses of only a few choice cuts of meat.

After the Atchison, Topeka, and Santa Fé railroad was driven through the center of the Southern herd (between 1866-1871), cities such as Dodge City became buffalo hunter outfitting centers and shipping stations. This further increased both the range and number of professional hide hunters. Besides the continuing over-kill and resultant waste of bison, another characteristic of the slaughter was becoming apparent, and this was the pleasure some people derived from killing bison merely for the psychological satisfaction of killing. This practice was not limited to hunters, but was shared by some settlers and towns-people alike. Wanting to serve the interests of the people the railroads occasionally sponsored special excursions during which passengers were given the opportunity to shoot from the windows of a standing train into the midst of a nearby bison herd. No part of the slaughtered animals was utilized.

The most intense killing of bison, particularly in the Southwestern United States, occurred between 1871 and 1874. At this time, hides could be sold for $1.25 apiece. For whatever reasons bison were being slaughtered, the accumulative killing almost exterminated the Southern herd. It is difficult to discuss the intensity of the killing during this period with complete accuracy. Some professional hunters and so-called sportsmen undoubtedly exaggerated their killing abilities. It is unlikely that precise records of the number of slaughtered-but-never-used bison were kept. However, in an account of his life on the plains, Colonel R. I. Dodge, an officer in the

United States Cavalry, estimated that white hunters had killed five buffalo for every hide that reached a market. This ratio of one to four resulted from poor marksmanship, skinning techniques, preservation methods, and from waste killing for psychological reasons.

The Atchison, Topeka, and Santa Fé was one of the few railroads that kept even partial records of their cargo, especially in terms of buffalo products transported. In 1872 the Atchison, Topeka, and Santa Fé carried to eastern markets approximately 275,000 buffalo robes and hides; and in 1873 the railroad transported an additional 251,000 robes and hides. It has been estimated that the Union Pacific and Kansas Pacific railroads together carried as many as 825,000 buffalo robes and hides between 1872 and 1873. Thus the railroads carried products from approximately 1,350,000 bison in a two year period. If Colonel Dodge's estimate that five animals were killed for every hide or robe that reached a market is correct, over 6,750,000 buffalo were slaughtered by white hunters between 1872 and 1873. In addition, author E. Douglas Branch estimates that, in the same time period, Indian hunters killed about 350,000 buffalo from the Southern herd, and that white farmers and ranchers killed thousands more for various reasons other than direct economic gain. This increases the estimate of the number of buffalo killed between 1872 and 1873 to 7,100,000 animals.

Remembering that the majority of the hides and meat were taken from slain cows, it is not hard to understand how, within a five year period, the buffalo population of the Southern herd was seriously threatened. By 1876 there were virtually no buffalo of the Southern herd left to commercially hunt; and by 1880 the last buffalo of the once great Southern herd was killed.

Long before the completion of the Northern Pacific railroad (between 1880-1882) influenced the slaughter of bison in the Northern herd, Indians and white hunter/trappers had established an annual trade for buffalo robes with the govern-

Courtesy Northern Pacific Railroad

A sketch of a Northern Pacific construction train stopped by a herd of buffalo—a common occurrence in the early days of western railroading. The drawing was made in 1875.

ment-chartered Hudson's Bay Company in Canada, and with individual firms such as the American Fur Company in the United States portion of the range. This trading annually brought in approximately 150,000 to 200,000 robes from the Northern herd. When the Northern Pacific railroad opened the hitherto unsettled lands of the northern Great Plains, the slaughter of the Northern herd greatly increased. Many of the hunters who had witnessed and aided in the demise of the Southern herd migrated north to continue their hunting where bison were still plentiful. In 1882, there were 5,000 or more white hide hunters and skinners actively searching out the buffalo of the Northern herd. Each hunter was evaluated on the basis of how many buffalo he could kill annually. If a hunter could not bring in 2,000 or more usable hides each year, he was considered to be a poor hunter.

As before, accurate records of the number of bison killed were not kept. By the 1880's the American public was becoming concerned about the rapidity with which the western

Pen drawing by Frederick Remington of a three-fourths buffalo calf.
Product of such crossing of cattle and buffalo were called cattalo.

bison were being killed. Thus, few hunting firms kept records
of the hides and robes purchased and sent eastward. There
are, however, a few tangible references which can be used as
indicators to reveal how many buffalo were killed between
1880 and 1883.

William Hornaday received a memorandum from the firm
of Joseph Ullman, fur buyers of New York, Chicago, and St.
Paul, indicating that this firm alone handled 14,000 hides and
12,000 robes in 1881.[5] In 1882, the firm purchased between
35,000 and 40,000 hides and approximately 10,000 robes. In
1883, the Joseph Ullman firm purchased only 6,000 to 7,000
hides and approximately 2,000 robes. The prices paid for these
hides and robes were as high as $2.50 to $4.00 apiece! Hornaday
also received reliable information from J. N. Davis, a fur buyer
of Minneapolis, estimating that the Northern Pacific railroad
shipped 50,000 hides in 1881; 200,000 hides in 1882; and
40,000 hides in 1883. Again accepting Dodge's contention that

[5] Although Mr. Hornaday's classic article on the extermination of
the buffalo has been much maligned because of exaggeration, incon-
sistencies, and, as suggested by some critics, his failure to obtain completely firsthand data, his work can still be used as a source of reference data.

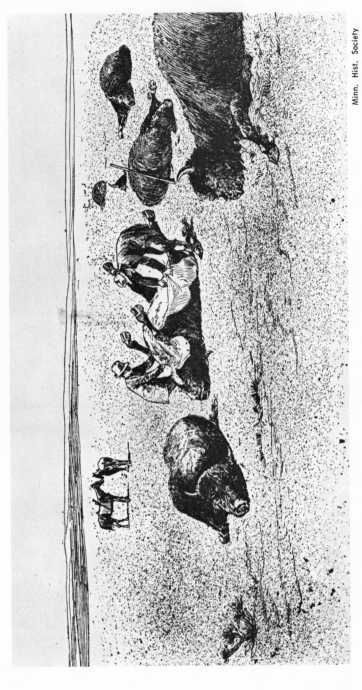

Caption of this drawing from the *Northwest Magazine*, 1890, read, "The game down, the work of the skinners began."

Buffalo skulls stacked eight feet high, and eight feet wide by two hundred feet long! These bones were shipped by Hugh Lumsden from Saskatoon to Minneapolis, Minnesota, at $5 to $7 a ton to be made into bone charcoal.

Hudson's Bay Co. "Beaver"

one hide or robe reached a market for every five bison killed, but allowing for the hunters to have become more efficient due to their experience in the Southwest, the total number of buffalo killed between 1880 and 1883 probably amounted to more than 12 million animals. In 1884 J. N. Davis shipped only one carload of robes from Dickinson, Dakota Territory. This was the last large shipment of buffalo hides or robes sent from the Great Plains.

Among the Canadian portion of the Northern herd, the slaughter was nearly over before 1880. The Cree, Blackfeet, and Beaver Indians had killed large numbers of bison for food as agriculture was difficult in the northern climate; and Indian and white hunters killed many more bison for trade with the Hudson's Bay Company. However, of greater importance to the livelihood of the bison in the Northern herd was that the Canadian government was alert to the need for protecting the Canadian buffalo herd from extinction—an idea the United States government did not share until it was almost too late to save the wild buffalo. Thus, after hunters had eliminated nearly all the buffalo of the American portion of the Northern herd, the Canadian portion remained more abundant, even though the Canadian herd was possibly only a few thousand in number.

Thus, within a span of sixty years, the greatest collection of mammals in the world had been nearly exterminated. Of the original 60 million bison that once freely roamed North America, there remained only those small groups or single buffalo in isolated areas immediately north of Lake Athabaska in Canada and in protected areas in the western United States. In 1887, there remained roughly 541 buffalo in the entire United States. Only 85 buffalo were known to be living in the wild state, 256 in captivity, and another 200 or so living under Federal management in Yellowstone National Park. Approximately 180 of the 541 buffalo were killed by poachers in Yellowstone National Park between 1887 and 1894. Of the free-roaming buffalo in Colorado, 60 were killed by poachers.

By 1894, there remained roughly 300 buffalo in the United States. Had it not been for the concern of men throughout the United States in the latter years of the nineteenth century who wished for the formal preservation of buffalo, the wild buffalo might well have become extinct.

References and Further Readings

Branch, E. Douglas. *The Hunting of the Buffalo*, Lincoln, Nebraska: University of Nebraska Press, 1962.

Dodge, R. I. *The Plains of the Great West*, New York: Archer House, 1959.

Gard, Wayne. *The Great Buffalo Hunt*, New York: A. A. Knopf, 1959.

Hornaday, W. T. "The Extermination of the American Buffalo," 1889.

McCreight, M. I. *Buffalo Bone Days*, Sykesville: Nupp Printing Co., 1939.

Roe, F. G. *The North American Buffalo*, Toronto: University of Toronto Press, 1970.

Sandoz, M. *The Buffalo Hunters*, New York: Hastings House, 1954.

Shoemaker, H. W. *A Pennsylvania Bison Hunt*, Middleburg: Middleburg Post Press, 1915.

Charlie Russell

Chapter Three

Conservation of the American Bison

Few late nineteenth century Americans were aware of the possible extinction of the reduced bison population. Objective reports and documents describing the slaughter were available to the public, such as J. A. Allen's article "The American Bisons, Living and Extinct" (1876), R. I. Dodge's book *The Plains of the Great West* (1877), and William T. Hornaday's article "The Extinction of the American Bison" (1889). However, most Americans preferred to learn about the buffalo through travelers' accounts, newspaper and magazine articles, and novelettes which often exaggerated and romanticized the killing. Detached Easterners, particularly, enjoyed the sense of adventure and excitement generated by such literature. Consequently, the carnage continued, for emotionalism obscured the realities of the slaughter and restricted early attempts to effectively retard and control the killing of bison.

Unlike the majority of Americans, people inhabiting the western territories often expressed deep concern over the decimation of the buffalo. Their proximity to the decreasing buffalo range made many Westerners keenly aware of the effects extermination of the buffalo could have on the nature and life of the plains.[1] In some territories, public concern ultimately influenced the enactment of legislation designed to protect and preserve the bison. In 1864 the Territory of Idaho outlawed the slaughter of buffalo. In 1871 the Territory of Wyoming made the slaughter of bison illegal. In 1872 penalities for hunters guilty of leaving meat to decay on the plains were established by the Territorial Legislature of Colorado. The Territory of Nebraska passed a law in 1875 intended to protect the buffalo, but the law was only a law of the books. Texas attempted to pass similar legislation; however, General Philip Sheridan, commander of the military department of the Southwest, convinced the legislators that such a protective measure was totally unnecessary and should, therefore, be avoided. The bill was never passed. Rather than pass laws explicitly protecting buffalo, the New Mexico and Dakota Territories passed game protection laws in 1880 and 1883, respectively. These laws provided protection for all wild animals, but by this time it was almost too late to save wild bison.

Although sincere in intent, these early efforts to protect the buffalo were futile. Bison hunters were seldom informed of the laws; and when informed, hunters disregarded the laws. The fines imposed on guilty hunters were usually small, and the civil means of enforcement was ineffectual. There were few marshals on the plains, and some of these marshals were also professional hide hunters whose attention to duty often conflicted with their vested interests as hunters!

On the national level, people from both the East and West, who were concerned with keeping the bison alive, reacted against the wanton killing of buffalo. As private citizens, organized groups, and government officials, these predecessors to our modern conservationists encouraged legislation

[1] Long after the decimation of the buffalo, researchers have contended that the buffalo did indeed alter the character of the plains. See F. Larson's "Role of the Bison in Maintaining the Short Grass Plains," *Ecology*, Vol. 21, 1940, pp. 113-121; and C. W. Johnson, "Protein as a Factor in the Distribution of the American Bison," *Geographical Review*, Vol. 41 (2), 1951, pp. 330-331.

intended to end the buffalo slaughter. In 1871 several federal legislators introduced bills in the Congress which would provide for the protection of buffalo.

The majority of Congress was not swayed by the pleas for the conservation of buffalo. Their opposition derived from: 1. a general lack of detailed, factual information concerning the slaughter of buffalo; 2. a general lack of interest and concern for the welfare of bison; and 3. the general fear that the preservation of buffalo would tend to perpetuate the problems whites were experiencing with the Plains Indians. In fact, the Secretary of the Interior under President Grant, Columbus Delano, contended that the Plains Indians could be easily subjugated by the federal government if bison were completely removed from the Great Plains, thereby depleting the Indians' basic source of food. Delano, therefore, hoped that hunters would not be restricted, but would eventually exterminate the wild bison.

Many of the proposed bills to protect and conserve the buffalo were far too vague to arouse congressional interest or action.[2] Consequently, the majority of all protective bills died in committee. Those few bills that were ultimately passed by the Congress were vetoed by the President; bills passed in the territorial legislatures, were vetoed by the governors. As a result, the years between 1871 and the early 1890's were characterized by the federal and territorial governments' inability to pass adequate laws to protect the buffalo on the western public lands.

Parks, Preserves, and Ranges

Despite the initial legislative impasse, significant events and attitude changes were taking place that ultimately eased

[2] For examples of the types of congressional bills proposed, see *Congressional Globe*, 1871-2, 42nd Congress, 1st Session and 2nd Session; *Congressional Record*, 1874, 43rd Congress, 1st Session; *Congressional Record*, 1876, 44th Congress, 1st Session; and an entire section devoted to the character of Congressional debate in W. T. Hornaday's "Extermination of the American Bison," 1889.

the way for more positive action to be taken for the conservation of buffalo. The earliest of these events was the concerted effort on the part of many organized people to conserve untouched portions of the United States as parks. Unlike the beginning of most organized movements, the wildlife refuge/ park movement seems to have no recorded originator. It appears that the time was right for people to become concerned with the preservation and protection of the United States's natural resources. Out of this concern came the first pioneer effort in American conservation—the establishment of Yellowstone National Park by the federal government in 1872.[3]

Bison were not indigenous to Yellowstone Park; however, as their numbers decreased throughout the plains area, the park provided the remaining buffalo with a final refuge. By the late 1890's, Yellowstone Park contained the largest single concentration of buffalo in the United States—over 200 animals. Unfortunately, the methods used to protect the buffalo within the park were weak and the penalties ineffectual. The specific regulation under which the United States Army was to manage the park stipulated little more than that the park should be protected. Violators were penalized merely by having their hunting equipment confiscated and by expulsion from the park. Second time offenders were not as well treated. They were often taken into a company corral where they were beaten sufficiently so as to inhibit any further incidents of poaching. Numerous attempts were made to strengthen the regulations protecting the park and its inhabitants, but the federal government refused to enact laws strong enough to protect all the game in the park, and particularly the bison. Thus, Yellowstone Park developed into a veritable hunter-poacher paradise.

During the winter of 1893-1894, 116 of the estimated 136 buffalo in Yellowstone Park were killed by professional

[3] For a short history of the wildlife refuge movement, see I. N. Gabrielson's *Wildlife Refuges*, New York: MacMillian Co., 1943. Also see Martin Garretson's *The American Bison*, New York: New York Zoological Society, 1938, for the story of Yellowstone National Park's buffalo under military protection.

poachers. News of this illegal killing, and the influential lobbying by sportsman-lawyer Hallet Phillips, finally convinced Congress that the buffalo did indeed need greater protection, at least in the national parks. In May, 1894, Congress passed the first substantial federal law protecting buffalo on any federally-owned land. The law, immediately signed by President Grover Cleveland, made it illegal to kill a bison, or any other animal, within the confines of Yellowstone National Park. Conviction was punishable by a fine of $1,000, imprisonment, or both.

With fewer than 20 buffalo remaining in Yellowstone Park in 1894, Charles J. Jones—better known as "Buffalo Jones"—a confirmed conservationist and owner of a private buffalo herd, began working to influence the Congress to appropriate funds for the acquisition of additional buffalo for the park. Eventually Congress responded to Jones' request. The additional bison were purchased from already existing privately-owned bison herds. In 1902 Congress named Jones the park superintendent, and provided funds for enlarging and protecting the buffalo herd. Jones used the appropriated $15,000 to purchase 18 pure-blood bison. Several additional bison were donated to the park by interested individuals.

Once the Yellowstone Park buffalo herd had become an investment, the government appropriated still more funds and established even more strict laws to conserve and maintain its commitments to the buffalo. In 1903, Congress made the first of an annual $2500 appropriation for the care of the Yellowstone Park buffalo herd. By 1910, Congress had increased the appropriation to $5000 per year; and by 1933 the amount was further increased to $11,000 to help pay for the care of the rapidly expanding bison herd. Until 1968, park officials maintained the Yellowstone Park herd at approximately 500 animals, believing this figure to be large enough for the park's purposes. But, since 1968, the park officials have decided to allow the herd to increase naturally until the buffalo population reaches the park's natural carrying capacity.

The establishment and success of the Yellowstone National Park buffalo herd set a precedent for the creation of additional national and state parks providing refuge for bison. Concomitantly, the federal government began manifesting a change in attitude toward Indians, thereby alleviating one of the major points of opposition to the conservation of buffalo. This change of attitude led to the opening of the Oklahoma-Kiowa-Comanche Reservation for settlement and to the establishment of a national forest reserve in 1901. In 1905 the reserve was designated a national game preserve by President Theodore Roosevelt; and, shortly thereafter, it was renamed the Wichita Mountain Wildlife Refuge.

In the early 1900's conservationists began working directly with the federal government to re-establish the buffalo population of the United States. Dr. William T. Hornaday, a naturalist, and a most active conservationist, contended that the only way bison in the wild state could be saved from extinction was to have the federal government establish and maintain several protected national bison reserves. Together with several other interested people, Hornaday organized the American Bison Society (ABS) to work toward this end. The Society's objective was the permanent preservation and increase of American bison in particular, and the protection of all North American big game in general.[4] The first organizational meeting was called to order on December 8, 1905, at the New York Zoological Park. Dr. Hornaday was elected president, for he had been an active leader in the fight for buffalo preservation for many years and his writings were known world-wide.

As president of the ABS, and director of the New York Zoological Society, Hornaday proposed that the New York Zoological Society provide the federal government with a nucleus herd of bison, if the government would appropriate sufficient monies to erect a fence around any reasonable grazing land within the Wichita Mountain Wildlife Refuge and to maintain that herd. In 1906 Congress agreed to the Society's offer.

[4] See Appendix C for a short history of the American Bison Society.

Fifteen of the New York Zoological Park's finest bison were set free in the refuge during that same year.

The first steps taken to establish an *exclusive* bison range were initiated by Congress in 1902 (H.R. No. 127). To assess the need for such a range, the secretaries of the Departments of the Interior and Agriculture were petitioned to assemble reports on the then current condition of buffalo herds in the United States. Both secretaries reported that a national bison range should be established, for the number of wild bison and pure-blood bison in the United States was seriously low.[5] In spite of the urgency of the secretaries' reports, further governmental action was delayed for six years.

In 1908 the Senate put forth a Senate bill (No. 6159) which called for the establishment of a national bison range on the Flathead Indian Reservation in Montana. Prior to this time, the owner of one of the largest privately-owned buffalo herds, an Indian named Michel Pablo, lived on the Flathead Reservation. However, by the time Congress finally acted to establish the National Bison Range, Pablo's herd had been dispersed through auction. Thus, the ABS felt obligated to provide the nucleus of animals for the National Bison Herd since the Congress had failed to act in time to preserve Pablo's bison. Dr. Hornaday requested donations for the purchase of buffalo for the range, and succeeded in raising approximately $10,500. In late 1909, the original herd of 34 buffalo was purchased from owners of private herds, and these animals were transported to the range. Several additional bison were donated by private owners.[6]

In 1912, the Niobrara National Wildlife Refuge was created near Valentine, Nebraska. Within a year, J. W. Gilbert offered to donate six of his buffalo with the stipulation that the animals would never be removed from the refuge.

[5] See Senate Documents Nos. 205 and 445, 1902, for the entire report of the Secretaries of the Interior and Agriculture.

[6] Today the number of bison that are kept on the National Bison Range number approximately 350, but some authorities feel the range is capable of supporting at least 900 animals.

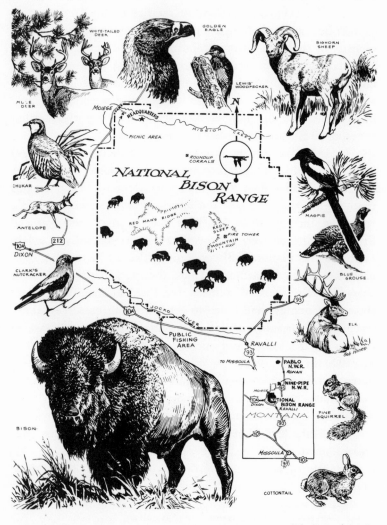

Back cover of a brochure describing the National Bison Range, showing the generous assortment of wildlife inhabiting the range.

The citizens of Valentine collected $2000 to have the refuge land fenced, and the six bison were turned free on the refuge in 1913. During the same year, Yellowstone National Park officials contributed two buffalo bulls to the small Niobrara herd.[7]

Wind Cave National Park in South Dakota was established in 1913 through the efforts of Franklin W. Hooper, then acting president of the American Bison Society. Again the ABS, and the New York Zoological Society, collaborated in providing a nucleus herd of 14 buffalo for the newly-created national park.[8]

Custer State Park in South Dakota, created in 1914, was the last of the large parks dedicated to the preservation of bison and other wildlife. The State of South Dakota purchased 25 buffalo, from Scotty Phillips, which were to be set free in the park. In 1951, an additional 60 buffalo were donated to the Custer State Park by the Sioux Indians.[9] Today Custer State Park owns one of the largest herds of buffalo in the United States with approximately 2000 head. The park is currently the only park in the nation that is completely self-sufficient. Its self-sufficiency is based primarily on the income from the annual sale of surplus buffalo and buffalo meat.

Thus, determined conservationists manipulated the indirect concern of the federal government toward the preservation of buffalo into the enactment of protective laws, and the appropriations of needed land and monies. By establishing and maintaining bison herds in designated parks, preserves, and refuges, conservation leadership in the state and federal governments was the most significant stimuli for an increased buffalo population in the early part of the twentieth century.

[7] The Niobrara National Wildlife Refuge supports some 300 buffalo.

[8] Wind Cave National Park remains one of the few areas of the Great Plains where primordial plains conditions are perpetuated and a herd of 250 buffalo is maintained to complete the natural balance.

[9] It is ironic that there should be a sufficient reversal in Indian-white relations so that Indians are now providing the white man with buffalo so that the animal might be preserved for posterity.

The Establishment of Privately Owned Bison Herds

The majority of buffalo herds in the United States today originated from privately-owned herds that were established between 1860 and 1910. Men of the West, like Charles Allard, Michel Pablo, Charles Conrad, Charles J. Jones, and Charles Goodnight, established the first private herds by capturing young, free-roaming bison, or by purchasing young animals from other bison raisers. These herds were developed primarily for conservation and personal interest. Owners seldom slaughtered their bison for profit. If profit was desired, it was usually obtained by selling live buffalo to individuals, private organizations, or government agencies which likewise evinced strong desire for the preservation and conservation of the animal.

Ownership of private herds, or portions of herds, was frequently transferred. The earliest transfers were between individuals who sought to either increase the size of their herd or prevent the inbreeding of their stock. Later, in the twentieth century, individuals such as Austin Corbin and Harry Trexler, who had developed an interest in buffalo for personal reasons, established private herds in the East as part of larger game preserves.[10] As the cost of land, taxes, and the requirements for the maintenance of buffalo herds have continued to increase throughout the years, many buffalo from the larger private herds have been donated to government agencies that promote, protect, and perpetuate the buffalo.

More recently, the symbolic nature of the buffalo has been an adjunct to conservation as a motivator of herd ownership. Small herds of from one to five animals have satisfied many bison raisers' desire to attach themselves to an element of the American heritage. To some the buffalo symbolizes the courage and perseverance that was necessary to "tame

[10] See Martin S. Garretson's book, *The American Bison*, for an in depth discussion of the most important early buffalo herds, their frequent changes in ownership, their interrelatedness, and their status as of 1938. Few of these original private herds exist today. See also E. T. Seton, Vol. 3, 1927, pp. 658-660; C. J. Jones, 1909, pp. 1-4; and E. H. Baynes, 1905, pp. 262-263.

the West;" to others the buffalo symbolizes man's responsibility to protect and preserve his natural environment. The impact of the symbolic nature of buffalo is made more apparent by the immortalization of the buffalo on the ten dollar bill, a 1923 and a 1970 postage stamp, and as part of numerous state flags and seals, e.g., the flags of Kansas and Wyoming. Until 1968, the seal of the Department of the Interior consisted of a buffalo bull standing on a prairie with mountains and the rising sun in the background. This seal was authorized

**UNITED STATES
DEPARTMENT OF THE INTERIOR**
FISH AND WILDLIFE SERVICE
BUREAU OF SPORT FISHERIES
AND WILDLIFE

and its design formulated between 1917 and 1956. The seal commemorated the symbolic act of conservation and signified the coordination of conservation groups under one federal department. In 1968, a new seal was designed for the Department of the Interior, consisting of two stylized hands to represent the new emphasis of the Department—ecology rather than merely conservation and preservation.

Conservation and the symbolic nature of the bison were once the primary stimuli for the perpetuation of the bison population. Today these reasons account for some of the largest and smallest bison herds in the United States. The largest herds are owned by the state and federal governments; the smallest are owned by individuals throughout the country. Nearly 48 percent of the present bison population, roughly 17,000 animals, is owned or administered to by 46 percent of

P. Stuckenschneider

Weathering skull of old buffalo which is fastened to a corral gate post at the National Bison Range. Excellent illustration of horn structure.

the bison raisers (including government agencies) for reasons of conservation and symbolism.[11]

It is unlikely that the present bison population will be significantly increased as a result of stimuli derived from a further desire for the conservation of buffalo or the animals' symbolic nature. The impetus for the creation of new parks and ranges for the protection of buffalo has diminished. The majority of established parks that do have buffalo have reached their biological carrying capacity, i.e., the total number of buffalo they can satisfactorily support under present park conditions of space and food. Consequently, the annual surplus of bison from established Parks are either slaughtered for their meat or sold alive to maintain healthy herds.[12] Finally, the small herds that are privately owned for their symbolic link with the American past account for proportionately few bison. If buffalo ever become so numerous so as to become a common creature, the importance of the symbolic nature of the bison will undoubtedly decrease.

Thus, due to the active work of conservationists in the late nineteenth and early twentieth centuries, the buffalo has been guaranteed a place in the parks, zoos, and in the heart of America. Never again will the buffalo be threatened with the possibility of extermination in the United States because of man's uncontrolled actions.[13]

[11] The figures used here, and throughout the remainder of this book, to describe the nature of the American buffalo herds and their owners are based on a random sampling of buffalo raisers throughout the United States. See Appendix A.

[12] In 1970, a total of 339 bison were sold at the National Bison Range, Moiese, Montana; the Niobrara National Wildlife Refuge near Valentine, Nebraska; and at the Wichita Mountain Wildlife Refuge, Cache, Oklahoma.

[13] It is interesting that the conservationists' influence on stimulating a larger American bison population will be minimal in the future, for attitudes have again changed. Today the buffalo has been preserved and protected. The issues of greatest concern now are those related to pollution of the air, seas, land, and water. Consequently, it must be people other than conservationists who will further stimulate an increase in the total number of buffalo in the United States in the twentieth century.

References and Further Readings

Bryan, P. "Man and the American Bison," *National Wildlife,* Vol. 2(1), 1963/1964, pp. 46-49.

Cahalane, V. H. "Restoration of Wild Bison," *Transactions of the North American Wildlife Conference,* Vol. 9, 1944, pp. 135-143.

Collins, H. H. *The Unvanquished Buffalo,* New York: Blue Heron Press, 1952.

The *Congressional Globe* and *Congressional Record,* Washington, D.C.: Government Printing Office. [There is a wealth of information in these records of Congressional debates, particularly between 1871 and 1905.]

Cook, J. R. *The Border and the Buffalo,* Topeka: Crane and Co., 1907.

Cross, J. M. "Dakotas Conserve Land and Buffaloes," *Farmland,* Vol. 36(6), 1969, pp. 1; 11.

Dodge, R. I. *The Plains of the Great West,* New York: G. P. Putnam's Sons, 1877 (Reprinted in 1959 by Archer House, Inc. under same title).

Elrod, M. J. "The Montana National Bison Range," *Journal of Mammalogy,* Vol. 7, 1926, pp. 45-48.

Garretson, M. S. *The American Bison,* New York: New York Zoological Society, 1938.

Literary Digest. "Bison Reappearing American," Vol. 99, 1928, pp. 70-74.

Stuckenschneider, N. "Will the Buffalo Roam . . . Again," *Record Stockman,* Vol. 80, 1969, pp. 148-149.

Chapter Four

The Influence of Economic Incentives on the Contemporary American Bison Population

Following the establishment of formal conservation of bison, the market for bison and bison products changed drastically. The seemingly endless supply of wild bison was gone; and owners of private herds had little or no interest in deriving economic gain from their animals. The resulting scarcity of bison available to the commercial market seemed to preclude the continuation of a large, lucrative market.

However, in the early 1900's, a market for bison products began to develop, characterized by a reversal in the animal's relative value. As people responded to the conservationists' encouragement for additional privately-owned bison herds, a well-paying market for live bison was created. Further, because public sentiment no longer allowed the waste that was common during the 1870-1890's, all bison products became more valuable, particularly the meat. Thus, although the bison market decreased in volume, the economic value of bison and bison products became far greater. This increased economic potential of the bison has motivated many people to raise bison explicitly for economic gain.

The Market for Live Bison

High and varied prices are characteristic of live bison sale transactions. This can be attributed to the relatively few bison available for sale and to contemporary interest in the animal.

The most common reasons people purchase live bison are: 1. for personal enjoyment or satisfaction; 2. to enlarge or improve the quality of already existing bison herds, frequently for economic gain; 3. to use bison to attract potential buyers to an economic concern; and 4. for use in scientific research.

Because of the informal nature of live bison sales, detailed information concerning the number of animals sold, and prices received, is generally lacking. However, there are sufficient records to show the price variability of bison transactions. In 1959, L. R. Houck of Pierre, South Dakota, purchased over 400 bison from Custer State Park, Hermosa, South Dakota, at a cost of $193,000.[1] Houck paid an average of $501 per cow and $360 per bull. Respondents to Questionnaire Form 2 have provided the following data: Walter H. Quast of Hutchinson, Minnesota, has sold bison cows for more than $400 apiece, calves for between $150 and $200 apiece, and a bull for as much as $600. In the late 1950's, Dewey Hebler of Moville, Iowa, purchased bison for approximately $250 per animal. As of 1968, he had received up to $275 per calf; between $400 and $550 per cow, and $700 for a fully matured bull. J. C. Oliver of O'Fallon, Illinois, likewise purchased his first bison for approximately $250 apiece and, in 1968, was offered considerably more than this amount for individual bison. Ray L. Wallace of Toledo, Washington, states that a week-old buffalo calf is worth $500; and by the time it is a two-year old, the buffalo is worth in excess of $1000.[2]

---

[1] This information was kindly given to the author by Mr. L. R. Houck of Pierre, South Dakota.

[2] Mr. Wallace's figure of $1000 appears to be somewhat high when compared with other data. This figure may represent a single unusual sale. However, Mr. Don Thompson of Manitowoc, Wisconsin, recently purchased a buffalo bull for $2000 in Nova Scotia. This buffalo, however, is a rarity, for the buffalo is extremely large when compared with most buffalo bulls. Jumbo, the buffalo's most appropriate name, weighs 3,340 pounds and is reportedly the largest of his kind in North America, or the world. Thompson suggests that Jumbo probably could bring up to $5,000 on the collector's market. The average price paid for bison on the open market seems to be roughly $450, depending on the animal, the buyer, and the section of the country.

Live buffalo are also sold annually at auctions held by the government parks, refuges, and preserves in order to maintain healthy herds at an optimum size. The details of these transactions again reveal a wide range of high prices. Despite the variability of prices received for buffalo, the prices paid are slightly higher than the average prices paid for domestic beef cattle which usually weigh several hundred pounds more. The average price paid for all cattle sold in 1969 was approximately $266 per animal according to the *1970 Agricultural Statistics* published by the U.S. Department of Agriculture. In comparison, the average prices paid for buffalo at the Wichita Mountain Wildlife Refuge auctions varied from $387.82 (1968); $464.53 (1969), to $377.60 (1970) (see Table 1, below). In only two instances during these auctions were the prices paid for buffalo less than that paid for domestic beef cattle.

TABLE 1 — Summary of Buffalo Auctions at the Wichita Mountains Wildlife Refuge, Cache, Oklahoma, 1968-1970

1968

Class	Age	No. Sold	Price Paid	Top Price	Average Price
Heifers	1½	36	$15,440	$490	$428
Bulls	1½	18	4,965	360	275
Heifers	2½	4	2,020	510	505
Bulls	2½	4	1,620	500	405
Totals for 1968		62	$24,045		$387.83

1969

Class	Age	No. Sold	Price Paid	Top Price	Average Price
Heifers	1½	38	$18,910	$535	$497.63
Bulls	1½	12	4,580	435	381.66
Heifers	2½	1	440	440	440.00
Bulls	2½	2	690	425	345.00
Totals for 1969		53	$24,620		$464.52

1970

Class	Age	No. Sold	Price Paid	Top Price	Average Price
Bulls	2½	11	$ 1,730	$175	$157.27
Bulls	3½	7	1,770	350	252.86
Heifers	1½	5	1,910	525	382.00
Heifers	2½	20	9,770	610	488.00
Heifers	3½	6	3,130	605	521.66
Heifers	4½	1	570 ·	570	570.00
Totals for 1970		50	$18,880		$377.60

Average Price Paid Per Animal, 1968-1970: $409.98

Between 1967 and 1969, the National and Historical Parks Branch of the Canadian government liquidated live bison from Elk Island National Park at Lament, Alberta. Any Canadian firm, or resident of Canada, interested in purchasing bison explicitly for ranching or the commercial production of bison meat and products were invited to submit sealed tenders. The Canadian government stipulated that bidders make prior arrangements for the maintenance and accommodation of the bison including; the erection of a barb-wire fence of at least five and a half feet high, arrangement for the transportation of the bison to a sizeable area of land, and full knowledge of a warning that although the bison could be pastured together with domestic stock, care must be taken to avoid hazardous cross-breeding.[3] In all cases the average prices received for

[3] No such stipulations have been placed on bidders at auctions held by any of the United States's bison preserves or parks. However, all the parks and preserves suggest that potential bison buyers read and acknowledge the requirements set forth in Wildlife Leaflet 212, *Buffalo Management*, published by the Bureau of Sport Fisheries and Wildlife, Division of Wildlife Refuges, in revised form, 1965. This leaflet suggests the minimum requirements for the enclosure of buffalo, forage and mineral requirements, a consideration of the growth and development of buffalo, and a synopsis of the major diseases and parasites which might affect the bison. See also Refuge Leaflet 413, *Surplus Animal Disposal on National Wildlife Refuges*, 1967, for more information on the availability and application procedures for the procurement of bison.

the Canadian buffalo were higher than the average prices paid for domestic cattle or calves (in 1969 the average price per calf was $64 according to the *1970 Agriculture Statistics*) (see Table 2, below).

TABLE 2 — Summary of the Canadian Auctions at the Elk Island National Park, 1967-1969

1967

Block	Composition	Minimum Price Asked	Price Received	Average Price
1.	25F, 2M	$2,700	$10,250	$500.00

1968

Block	Composition	Minimum Price Asked	Price Received	Average Price
1.	22F, 3M (Calves)	$2,500	$ 7,525	$301.00
2.	22F, 3M (Calves)	2,500	5,500	220.00
3.	20M (Calves)	2,000	No Acceptable Bid	
4.	19M (Calves)	1,900	1,520	79.50
5.	20F, 3M (1 yr.)	2,300	7,610	328.00
6.	25M (1 yr.)	2,500	3,500	140.00
7.	25M (1 yr.)	2,500	3,500	140.00
8.	13M (2 yrs.) & 10M (1 yr.)	2,300	3,243	142.00
Totals	165		$32,398	$195.75

1969

Block	Composition	Minimum Price Asked	Price Received	Average Price
1.	16F, 3M (Calves)	$1,900	$ 4,465	$235.00
2.	16F, 3M (Calves)	1,900	4,229.13	264.31
3.	12M (Calves)	1,200	1,200	100.00
4.	12M (Calves)	1,200	1,020	89.50
Totals	62		$10,914.13	$111.11

Average Price Paid Per Animal, 1967-1969: $268.95

The Characteristics of the Bison Meat Market

An overwhelming majority (82 percent) of the respondents to Questionnaire Form 2 stated that raising bison is financially rewarding. Over 37 of those who qualified their affirmation stated that the prosperity of bison management is in the ease of selling bison meat as a health food, novelty, or promotional device. However, a few bison raisers, such as Stanley Herrling of Cross Plains, Wisconsin, do not agree. Herrling suggests that the future of the bison market lies in the sale of breeding stock, "...as the public will, in most cases, reject an 'unusual' meat like bison for their [the public's] bland, common, everyday plate of beef."

The market for bison meat is presently active only on a limited scale. The majority of the meat reaches the open market through small privately-owned restaurants, the Durham Meat Company, and individual Safeway chain food stores. Although not as elaborately developed as present outlets for beef cattle, outlets for bison are continually increasing as suggested by Questionnaire Form 2.

A long standing debate exists between bison and cattle raisers concerning the ability of their respective animals to produce nearly equal amounts of commercially valuable meat. The debate has remained unsettled, for it has been based primarily on unempirical information and unsystematic experience. Below is the empirical evidence revealing that bison are capable of producing greater quantities of meat, with less waste and supervision, than domestic beef cattle.

A. A Comparison of Bison and Domestic Beef Cattle in Meat Production

American bison are ruminants. Like cattle, they can digest bulky fodder; unlike cattle, they can survive on much less, but equally nutritious food. Common beef cattle are best suited to succulent grasses which are frequently watered by nature or irrigation systems. Cattle also require large amounts of water and, often, need supplements added to their diet of pasture grasses. Contrastingly, bison seem to thrive on short, dry grasses and require water only every three or four days. This is advantageous to the bison, for short grasses generally have a larger proportion of protein to roughage (cellulose) than do the larger grazing plants. On maturing and drying, short grasses maintain their high protein ratio, containing approximately 15 to 20 percent protein and 75 to 80 percent roughage. Protein plays a dominant role as the major constituent of an animal's body cells and must, therefore, be constantly renewed at a rate equal to the body's requirements for cellular maintenance. If a ratio of approximately 1:6, protein to fuel foods (carbohydrates, fats, etc.), is not maintained in an animal's diet for extended periods of time, the animal could die of starvation at the cellular level. An animal cannot always compensate for protein deficiency by eating greater quantities of food. Thus, both the quality and quantity of food must be maintained at a rate that will provide the animal with the correct ratio of protein to fuel foods. Short grasses seem more than adequate for the buffalo in this regard.

A bison weighing approximately 1000 pounds and grazing on grasslands requires approximately 30 pounds of food per day, or 900 pounds per month. This rate of consumption represents an average intake of three percent of the bison's live weight per day. Domestic beef cattle, of similar weight and subsisting on a similar range, would require an average of approximately 35 to 38 pounds of food per day, or 180 pounds per month more than a bison. This rate of intake would represent approximately 3.6 percent of the cattle's live weight.[4]

In an experiment conducted at Manyberries, Alberta, Canada, during 1952-53 and 1956-57, the feedlot requirements

[4] The figures cited here are only estimates. Palmer did not have the necessary facilities to subject buffalo to scientifically controlled circumstances. When cattle are being finished in feedlots, they consume feeds in amounts (daily air-dry basis) equal to approximately 3.6 percent of their live weight. The percentage varies as the concentrate-roughage ratio, age, and condition of the animal fluctuates.

for bison, hybrid, and Hereford calves were empirically compared.[5] At the conclusion of the experiment, the bison exhibited an average daily and total gain in pounds less than that for the Hereford,[6] but the quality of the meat from these animals was very similar. The bison did not consume as much food as the Hereford, but showed a substantially higher rate of utilization of total digestible nutrients per unit gain. The average dressing percentage (the weight of the carcass as it would be prepared for a cold storage locker) for the bison was higher than that for the Hereford, although the average percentage of carcass weight in the hindquarters was somewhat smaller for the bison (see Table 3, page 73). It appears that Hereford have heavier hides, viscera, heads, tails, and hooves than do bison which could account for the differences in dressed weights. The results of this experiment suggest that, while the bison is not as fast developing overall, it is capable of putting more meat on its body with less food during a given amount of time than is the Hereford.[7]

From 1953 to 1956, Arthur Halloran kept records of the bison annually culled from the herd at the Wichita Mountain Wildlife Refuge. See Tables 4 and 5 on pages 74 and 75, respectively, for Halloran's records of the age, average dressed

[5] This experiment was under feedlot conditions. Therefore, the results can only suggest differences between buffalo and Hereford as to food requirements on the open range for each.

[6] Individual beef cattle of conventional types gain weight at a fairly constant rate up to 900 or 1000 pounds. When this weight has been reached, gains decrease as maturity is approached. As cattle become heavier, a high proportion of the feed consumed is required for maintainance and apparent weight-gain efficienty is reduced. See Cole, 1962, pp. 244-246 for further information.

[7] In W. Gentry's 1916 article, Gordon W. Lillie, an early buffalo raiser, is quoted: "Buffalo can be raised economically. They thrive on pasture, need no pampering, required practically no attention and fatten rapidly in the fall on a little alfalfa. The money received from the meat, robes, and mounted heads is almost net. I don't know of any cattle business returning greater profits." Dr. Dwain W. Cummings, chairman of the Research Committee of the N.B.A., states that buffalo have been reported "...to gain 5 pounds a day, whereas...domestic beef are considered good if they gain 2½ pounds a day." Don Murphy of Eatonville, Washington, states: "A buffalo in a feedlot will gain 4½ pounds a day to a beef's average gain of 2¾ pounds a day."

TABLE 3 — Feedlot Performance and Carcass Characteristics of Bison and Hereford Calves at Manyberries, Alberta, 1952-53 and 1956-57[a]

	Exp. No.	Males		Females	
		Bison	Herefords	Bison	Herefords
No. of animals in Test	1	9	11	8	10
	2	8	10	11	10
Average initial weight (lbs.)	1	343	371	331	382
	2	377	388	366	375
Average daily gain (lbs.)	1	1.4	2.0	1.1	1.8
	2	1.1	2.4	0.9	2.1
Average daily feed intake (lbs.): Hay	1	3.1	3.5	3.7	4.2
Grain	1	9.0	11.5	9.5	11.6
Hay	2	2.9	4.7	2.7	4.6
Grain	2	8.7	12.6	8.0	12.3
T.D.N./lb. gained*	1	594	496	787	578
	2	700	477	831	534
Average dressing Percentage	1	60.1	59.8	61.7	58.0
	2	60.1	58.5	59.8	56.1
Average Carcass grade**	1	S	Dl	M	A
	2	S	S	Dl	A
Average percent of carcass weight in the hind-quarters	1	46.1	48.2	47.6	49.3
	2	46.8	47.8	47.5	50.4

*—Total Digestible Nutrients
**—A-Choice, B-Good, C-Commercial, Dl-Utility, M-Canners and Cutters, S-Bully.

a (After Peters, 1958, p. 88)

73

TABLE 4 — Live and Dressed Weights of American Bison taken from 1953-1956 at Wichita Mountain Wildlife Refuge, Cache, Oklahoma[a]

Bulls:

Age in Years	Average Dressed Weight (lbs.) (Weight-range)	No. of Animals Weighed	Average Live Weight (lbs.) (Weight-range)	No. of Animals Weighed	Percent of Yield
1	370	1	*	*	*
2	450 (393-518)	36	865 (795-995)	18	53
3	504 (426-580)	49	968 (945-1150)	24	52
4	616 (383-775)	22	1163 (925-1300)	8	53
5**	680 (531-827)	11	1138 (895-1315)	6	60
6	689 (596-899)	13	1273 (1015-1599)	3	54
7	789 (779-798)	2	1525	1	52
8	784 (672-897)	5	*	*	*
9	870 (811-929)	2	*	*	*
10	811 (788-834)	2	*	*	*
11	799 (738-869)	3	*	*	*
12	821	1	*	*	*
14	743	1	*	*	*

*—No Data
**—Average age at which bison reach maturity.

a (Halloran, 1957, p. 139).

74

TABLE 5 — Live and Dressed Weights of American Bison taken from 1953-1956 at Wichita Mountain Wildlife Refuge, Cache, Oklahoma[a]

Cows:

Age in Years	Average Dressed Weight (lbs.) (Weight-range)	No. of Animals Weighed	Average Live Weight (lbs.) (Weight-range)	No. of Animals Weighed	Percent of Yield
1	329	1	*	*	*
2	468 (431-534)	7	930 (876-985)	2	50
3	472 (408-538)	13	858 (820-990)	8	55
4	482 (421-547)	25	891 (850-950)	11	54
5	476 (420-530)	11	877 (800-945)	6	54
6	500 (453-557)	8	862 (857-870)	3	58
7	500 (461-542)	4	930	1	54
8	520 (484-557)	7	949 (940-1020)	6	55
9	524 (457-590)	2	945	1	55
11	469 (467-471)	2	*	*	*
12	473 (434-500)	4	872 (800-910)	4	54

*—No Data

[a] (Halloran, 1957, p. 139).

TABLE 6 — The Dressed Carcass Weight by Age Groups of Bison from Wood Buffalo National Park, 1961[a]

Age (Years)	Sex	Size Sample	Dressed Carcass Weight Mean	Range
Calf	M	6	137	101-178
	F	3	138	106-165
1½	M	3	230	186-282
	F	10	230	190-271
2½	M	24	407	299-539
	F	9	395	291-464
3½	M	6	583	438-655
	F	8	453	403-500
4½	M	1	757	*
	F	6	480	403-537
5½	M	4	783	629-953
	F	2	521	494-548
6½	M	1	818	*
	F	1	503	*
8½	M	3	769	746-790
	F	0	*	*
9½	M	2	801	767-835
	F	0	*	*
12½	M	0	*	*
	F	2	467	448-486
16½	M	0	*	*
	F	2	515	508-522
18½	M	1	950	*
	F	3	*	441-476

* No Data   [a] (After Novakowski, 1965, p. 176)

TABLE 7 — Weight and Value of the Carcass and Non-carcass parts of cattle expressed as percentages of the weight and value of the live animal[a]

Item	% Live Weight	% Live Value
Hide	6.0 - 11.0	4.6
Feet	1.3 - 1.8	0.1
Heart	0.3 - 0.5	0.3
Caul Fat	0.0 - 3.0	0.3
Liver	0.9 - 1.2	0.8
Lungs	0.9 - 1.3	0.2
Kidneys	0.4 - 0.6	0.2
Head:		
Tongue	0.2 - 0.4	0.3
Head and		
Cheek meat	0.3 - 0.5	0.4
Head Bones	2.3 - 2.5	0.2
Remaining Vicera	17.0 - 28.0	2.6
Carcass, dressed	50.0 - 62.0	89.7

[a] (Cole, 1962, p. 39)

weights, average live weights, and percent yield of meat from live bison (see Table 6, page 76, for additional dressed carcass weights of bison by age groups).

According to Ashbrook and Levie, the carcass of beef animals (less the head, hide, feet, and viscera) is between 40 and 65 percent of the live weight of the animals, with an average of approximately 54 percent. A comparison of this average with Tables 4 and 5 indicates that in only two instances was the percent of carcass yield from the live weight of bison bulls[8] equal to or greater than that for the average beef cattle.

[8] The buffalo subsisted on grass without being given feed supplements of hay. If placed on feedlots similar to those for domestic cattle, bison are capable of producing an average of 60 percent yield of meat for bulls and 57 percent for cows. This indicates that buffalo could surpass most domestic cattle (Hereford) in the production of meat if given equal care and attention.

Harry Pon of Arcadia, California, states that buffalo bulls which he has sold dressed out at 57 percent of their live weight. Don Hight of Murdo, South Dakota, states that his bison dress out at approximately 56 percent of their live weight.

Figure 1 — Wholesale Cuts and Percentage of Each on a Live Basis[a]

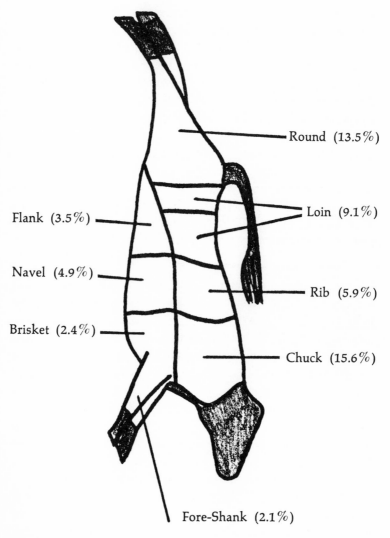

Round (13.5%)

Loin (9.1%)

Flank (3.5%)

Navel (4.9%)

Rib (5.9%)

Brisket (2.4%)

Chuck (15.6%)

Fore-Shank (2.1%)

Head, Hooves, and Tail (almost no wholesale value)—grey areas.

[a] (After Cole, 1962, p. 38)

However, bison cows dressed out equal to or above the average beef cattle in eight out of nine groups. This suggests that, for nearly all age groups, bison are able to produce an equal, if not greater, percentage of meat than are cattle.

The only significant factor adversely affecting the bison's economic importance is that the grade of bison is somewhat lower than the grade of beef, particularly in yearlings. However, many individuals have suggested that bison meat tastes like beef except that bison meat is slightly darker, more tender, smaller grained, and has a lower rate of cholesterol.

The bison, then, is adapted to thriving on seemingly poor ranges which common domestic beef cattle are unable to efficiently utilize. Further, it appears that the bison is capable of producing meat nearly equal to that of beef in quality, and greater in quantity, with less supervision by man. Thus, the bison has the potential to be raised commercially and return generous economic profits for its meat.

B. Economic Returns for Bison Meat

The economic returns received for the sale of bison meat are relatively high compared with returns for similar cuts of domestic beef (see Figure 2, page 80; and Table 8, page 82). However, the price received for bison meat is extremely variable due to the nature of the bison/bison product supply-market (or demand complex). This complex both aids and hinders bison raisers, depending on the size of their herd. That is, many owners of small herds find the markets closed to them because the owners cannot supply sufficient quantities of meat to the various outlets. However, if these bison raisers increased the size of their herds to overcome this problem, the price received for bison would drastically decline.

During the Second Annual Meeting of the National Buffalo Association (N.B.A.) in 1969, discussion was directed toward the price standards to which the membership should strive in selling bison meat. Armando Flocchini, manager of the Durham Meat Company of San Jose, California, one of

Figure 2 — Retail Cuts of Beef*

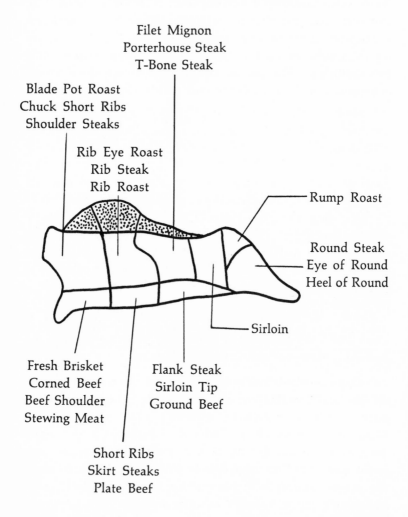

Filet Mignon
Porterhouse Steak
T-Bone Steak

Blade Pot Roast
Chuck Short Ribs
Shoulder Steaks

Rib Eye Roast
Rib Steak
Rib Roast

Rump Roast

Round Steak
Eye of Round
Heel of Round

Sirloin

Fresh Brisket
Corned Beef
Beef Shoulder
Stewing Meat

Flank Steak
Sirloin Tip
Ground Beef

Short Ribs
Skirt Steaks
Plate Beef

* The stippled area represents the "hump" of the bison in relation to the various retail cuts of beef. The hump is the result of the extension of the dorsal vertebrae. It provides a greater quantity of the higher priced commercial cuts of meat than is possible for domestic beef cattle.

the largest packers of bison meat, presented recommendations for uniform prices on a national scale (see Table 9, page 82). Flocchini requested that all members of the N.B.A. send the average prices received for bison or bison meat to the secretary of the association so that an equitable pricing system could be established. The system would then be submitted to the membership as a possible national pricing procedure.

Many of the bison breeders present at the 1969 N.B.A. meeting suggested that a cooperative marketing association be established to overcome the difficulty of selling limited quantities of bison to available buyers. It appears that most chain operated food stores dealing in bison meat prefer to purchase a minimum of 40,000 pounds per shipment, or at least 60 to 70 head at a time; most would prefer shipments of up to 400 head at a time. At present no individual breeder is able to provide the market with more than 200 head at one time. Nevertheless, the economic returns for bison meat continue to stimulate ownership of small herds of from 10 to 25 animals for economic gain.

Costs and Considerations of Obtaining, Maintaining, and Preparing Bison for the Consumer Market

Costs of obtaining, maintaining, and preparing bison for the consumer market are necessary concerns to people interested in raising buffalo for economic gain. Gibbons Clark states that a person can profitably raise bison on a commercial basis with a minimum herd of 100 animals. Expressing a different view, Dr. Cutting B. Favour, director of Medical Education at San Francisco's St. Mary's Hospital and Medical Center, states: "To my knowledge no large operator has yet run a herd of less than 1000 head of bison profitably." Favour belives it is impractical for people raising small herds of buffalo to market buffalo commercially due to the proportionately high costs of implementing the increasing number of health regulations, e.g., brucellosis certification. To be commercially profit-

TABLE 8 — A Comparison between the Price Received for
Commercial Cuts of Meat from Bison (as of
December 8-10, 1968) and from Beef (as of June
9-14, 1969).

Type of Meat	Consumer Cost Per Pound Bison[9]	Beef[10]
Boneless Steaks:		
Tenderloin and Sirloin	$3.40-3.50	$1.98
Steaks with a Bone:		
T-Bone and Porterhouse	2.65-2.75	1.19
Chuck Roasts	.88	.89
Short Ribs	.89	.49
Stew Meat	1.25	.89
Ground Round	.90	.99
Flank Steak	1.50	1.19
Chuck Steak	.88	.69
Ground Chuck	.89	.79
Hamburger	1.25	.59
Boneless Roasts	1.90-2.00	
Cube Steak	1.65-1.75	
Smoked Tongue	.90-1.00	
Buffalo Sampler (10 lb. assortment)	22.50-25.00	

[9] The prices for bison were obtained from the Durham Meat Company, San Jose, California.
[10] The prices for beef were obtained from the Lone Star Meat Company, Austin, Texas.

TABLE 9 — A Comparison of Consumer and Dealer Costs
for Bison Meat.

Type of Meat	Consumer Cost Per Pound	Dealer Cost Per Pound
Steaks - Rib and T-Bone	$3.00	$2.50
Sirloin, Tenderloin, and New York Cuts	3.50	3.00
Roasts - Cafeteria Round	1.50	1.00
Boneless (rolled and tied)	2.00	1.50
Bone in Chuck	1.50	1.00
Hamburger	1.25	.75
Stew Meat	1.50	1.25
Flank Steak	1.50	1.25

able, Favour believes one must own an operation consisting of more than 50,000 acres of range; 2000 to 5000 bison; six-foot-high fences; weaning pastures; special holding corrals (heavier than are necessary for domestic cattle); weighing, cutting, branding, and tagging facilities; carcass analysis and record keeping facilities; and possibly computer-controlled data information. This is not to say that economic gain need be predicated on the raisers' facilities as suggested by Favour. The majority of bison raisers in the United States have, at one time or another, experienced the highly profitable nature of the present bison market without such elaborate facilities.

Harry Pon, owner of the largest private bison herd in the United States, reports that the annual cost of raising a single bison is approximately $100. This figure is based on the operating overhead, i.e., mortality rates, real estate, personal and property taxes, interest on investments, etc. Private owner Don Hight projects this figure to $300 for raising and maintaining a bison until maturity is reached at age three. Finishing a bison can be hastened by keeping the bison on grassy ranges for two years, followed by approximately 70 to 90 days of finishing on a feedlot. At the end of this period, the animal should weigh approximately the same as a three-year-old reared under less supervised conditions.

The costs of raising and maintaining disease-free cattle is often prohibitive to owners of small herds. Bison, on the other hand, eliminate these stifling costs by being relatively disease-free when compared to beef cattle. An overwhelming plurality of the respondents to Questionnaire Form 2 replied that they had experienced no problems with their herds because of disease. Nevertheless, without proper care and certain precautions, bison are susceptible to certain disease.

Respiratory tuberculosis is the most common variety of "TB" found in bison. It is often difficult to control the spread of tuberculosis in an infected herd because the gregarious behavior of bison acts to maintain the disease. There are several developmental stages of tuberculosis, progressing from the initial infection to the late generalization when vital organs are infected and death is inevitable. It is usually not until late generalization begins that the animal is considered unsafe for human consumption. The various strains of tuberculosis can live in dead muscle only seven to nine days. Consequently, the meat from a tuberculous bison is safe for human consumption after this time period unless there is evidence of massive infection.

Tuberculosis is rapidly declining in the bison herds of the United States due to state and federal eradication programs. Only one of 144 replies to question 3, Questionnaire Form 2, indicated that tuberculosis had ever been a problem. This is not to say that tuberculosis is not found in bison herds throughout the United States, but that the occurrence of the late generalization stage is very rare.

Brucellosis, or "Bang's disease" is very common among both bison and cattle of the United States. When brucellosis infects bison bulls, the testes often become enlarged and abscessed. In bison cows, the bacteria affect the supramammary lymph nodes and uterine abscesses occur causing abortions when the disease first infects the cow.

According to Stan Stenson, Park Ranger at Custer State Park, brucellosis is not exceedingly serious for bison. A year after brucellosis infects a herd, the bison seem to adapt to the disease and further symptoms are rare. There is no point at which cattle adapt to brucellosis. Cattle remain infected and abortions continue indefinitely until the disease is treated and cured. With bison, the disease may spread through a herd until approximately 50 percent of the animals are infected. This appears to be the saturation level for the disease. As far as is known, brucellosis does not, in any way, affect the meat-producing potential of bison, nor does it affect the quality of the meat to the extent that the meat would be inedible. Custer State Park bison are annually vaccinated against brucellosis to prevent the occurrence of abortions. This practice seems to be quite common among bison raisers.

Internal parasites were considered to be the greatest pathological problem that questionnaire respondents have had to overcome in their bison herds. Wild bison exhibit few maladies that can be traced to internal parasites; however, several types can be found among domestic bison herds.[11] The internal parasites appear to cause more discomfort than danger if the infected animal is treated immediately upon manifestation of symptoms.

Bison are surprisingly free from external parasites. However, the tick *Dermacentor andersoni* can produce a dangerous disease known as "tick paralysis." Occurrence of tick paralysis among bison is extremely low.

Other diseases known to affect bison are blood worms, "pinkeye," "foot rot," anthrax, arthritis, arteriosclerosis, and temporary diarrhea resulting from the change from dry feed to new grass in the spring.

In the final analysis, few parasites and diseases have proven fatal to bison if the herds are maintained under sanitary conditions, if precautions are taken to guard against the purchase of infected animals, and if herds are periodically subjected to tests for disease and parasites by qualified veterinarians. Thus, if the overall conditions in which bison live are sanitary, bison raisers should have no problems with

[11] *Haemonchus contortus*, or "stomach worms," *Moniezia benedeni*, a species of tapeworm, and *Dictyocaulus viviparus*, or lungworms, are the most common worms known to affect buffalo. If not treated upon manifestation of the symptoms common to each worm, all may cause death for the infested animal.

Hypoderma larvae have been found in the muscle layer surrounding the esophagus and in the back beneath the buffalo's hide. The larvae are relatively common in buffalo, but cause little problem to the livelihood of the animal.

Liver flukes seldom cause serious disorder or discomfort to bison, although acute cases usually bring sudden death.

Scours, is the worst disease affecting buffalo calves of less than a month. The animal becomes weak and tends to lose its appetite. Scours can be prevented by feeding the calves small, daily amounts of terramycin and aureomycin. Concentrated doses of these antibiotics can cure an already infected calf when carefully administered by a qualified veterinarian.

diseases and parasites and, accordingly, should experience no problems in selling bison or bison meat because of the same.

Transporting finished bison to the slaughter house is more expensive than transporting domestic beef cattle. The temperament of bison does not allow them to be closely confined during transport as is the case with cattle. If crowded into a cattle truck, bison will hook and gore one another, thereby reducing the wholesale price the bison owner will receive for the injured animals. In their book, *Beef Production*, Diggins and Bundy state that annual losses sustained by the livestock industry because of damaged carcasses run into millions of dollars. Most of this damage could be prevented if the raisers would refrain from over-crowding, and from careless and abusive handling during transport. The same is true for bison raisers. Thus, if a cattle truck has a capacity of 25 to 30 domestic cattle, an average of only 10 to 15 bison should be transported in the same truck. Realizing the many liabilities involved, many truckers will not transport bison unless the seller pays above the standard fee required for cattle transport and provides his own insurance on both the truck and the animals.

The cost of slaughtering and processing bison is often slightly higher than it is for domestic beef cattle. Depending on the individual firm, the cost of slaughtering bison varies from $10 to as much as $30 per head. The cost for processing varies from $8 per hundred pounds of processed meat to approximately $12 per hundred pounds.

Thus, the overall costs of transporting and slaughtering live bison, and for processing and delivering bison meat to retailers is approximately $10 per animal higher than it is for domestic beef cattle.

Other Economically Valuable Bison Products

In addition to meat, several other valuable products can be obtained from bison. Hides prepared as "buffalo blankets" sell for from $150 to $200 apiece. Hides in the raw state sell for from $12 to $50. Heads, which can be mounted as trophies, or bleached and mounted as interior decorations, sell for from $80 to $200 apiece. The feet can be made into cigarette lighters which sell for from $5 to $20, and horns can be sold for from $5 to $10 a set.

Bison "wool" has proven to be valuable on an extremely limited scale. Around the beginning of the twentieth century, Charles Goodnight of Texas collected bison wool that he then had milled into blankets. Much more recently, Howard Miller, retired Congressman from the 1st District, Kansas, had several rugs woven by Navajoes from bison wool. On the basis of this experience, Miller states that there is "...room here for a worthwhile industry. I hope to procure more wool and try it again." The primary obstacle in marketing bison wool is the methods required for taking the wool from the bison. The animal's superior strength makes shearing an extremely tedious and dangerous process. Thus, although the bison's pelage is often longer than two inches and easily spun or woven, it is unlikely that a large-scale bison wool industry will ever develop.

Today the limited supply of animals enables bison and their products to be sold at prices that are economically rewarding to bison raisers. On the other hand, because bison are relatively scarce, they remain unfamiliar to the majority of contemporary Americans. Few people are aware that bison can thrive on pasturage unfit for domestic beef cattle; that, under similar conditions, bison gain weight more efficiently than cattle; or that the ratio of edible meat to waste products is higher for bison than for cattle. In spite of these advantages of bison over cattle, and the similar taste of bison meat and beef, bison have not yet begun to compete with beef in the commercial food market. Few people have attempted to utilize the full meat-producing potential of the bison. Today only 40 percent of the total population is directly related to the commerical market for live bison and their numerous products.

The supplying of this national market involves only 17 percent of all bison raisers.

Owners of large, commercially oriented herds are striving to increase the bison population in the hope of making bison products more familar to the general public, as well as economically competitive with beef. Concommitantly, numerous owners of small herds are resisting attempts to increase the bison population for fear that this would lower the value for their live bison and bison meat. Nevertheless, considering the present commerical value of bison and the apparent growth in the bison market, economic incentives represent the greatest potential stimuli for the future increase of captive bison.

References and Further Readings

Bergstrom, R. C. "Sheep Liver Fluke, Fasciola hepatica L. 1758 from Buffalo in Western Wyoming," *Journal of Parasitology*, Vol. 53(4), 1967, p. 724.

Bylin, J. E. "Some Restaurants Add a Buffalo Bill of Fare and People Eat it Up," *The Wall Street Journal* (4 December), 1968.

Cameron, A. E. "Notes on Buffalo: Anatomy, Pathological Conditions, and Parasites," *Veterinary Journal*, Vol. 79, 1923, pp. 331-336.

Cole, H. H., Ed. *Introduction to Livestock Production*, San Francisco: W. H. Freeman and Co., 1962.

Creech, G. T. "Brucella abortus Infection in Male Bison," *North American Veterinarian*, Vol. 11(1), 1929, pp. 35-36.

Diggins, R. V. and Bundy, C. E. *Beef Production*, Englewood Cliffs, New Jersey: Prentice Hall, 1962.

Dikmans, G. "New Records of Helminth Parasites," *Proceedings of the Helminthal Society of Washington*, Vol. 1(2), 1934, pp. 63-64.

Frick, E. J. "Parasitism in Bison," *Journal of the American Veterinary Medical Association*, Vol. 119(896), 1951, p. 387.

Gentry, W. "Buffalo for the Market," *Country Gentleman*, Vol. 81, 1916, p. 1900.

Hadwen, S. "Tuberculosis in the Buffalo," *Journal of the American Veterinary Medical Association*, Vol. 100(778), 1942, pp. 19-22.

Halloran, A. F. "Live and Dressed Weights of American Bison," *Journal of Mammalogy*, Vol. 38(1), 1957, p. 139.

Jellison, W. L., *et. al.* "An Outbreak of Tick Paralysis in Cattle in Western Montana," *Veterinary Medicine*, Vol. 46, 1951, pp. 163-166.

Locker, B. "Parasites of Bison in Northwestern USA," *Journal of Parasitology*, Vol. 39(1), 1953, pp. 58-59.

McNary, D. C. "Anthrax in American Bison," *Journal of the American Veterinary Medical Association*, Vol. 112(854), 1948, p. 378.

Palmer, L. J. "Food Requirements of Some Alaskan Game Animals," *Journal of Mammalogy*, Vol. 25(1), 1944, pp. 49-54.

Peters, H. F. "A Feedlot Study of Bison, Cattalo and Hereford Calves," *Canadian Journal of Animal Science*, Vol. 38, 1958, pp. 87-90.

Rush, W. M. "Bang's Disease in the Yellowstone National Park Buffalo and Elk Herds," *Journal of Mammalogy*, Vol. 13(4), 1932, pp. 371-372.

Sheng, T. S. "Virus Encephalomeylitis in Buffaloes," *Science*, Vol. 103, 1946, p. 344.

Tait, W. M. "New Source of Wool Supply in Canada, a Buffalo," *Farmers' Advocate*, Vol. 55, 1920, p. 1568.

Shooting buffalo from the trains of the Kansas Pacific Railroad. Sketched by Theodore R. Davis.

Harper's Weekly, 1867

Chapter Five

Novelty

Early in the nineteenth century, the millions of bison roaming the Great Plains caused Americans of the eastern United States to look upon the abundance of live bison as a novelty. At this time, the excitement generated by the novelty of the bison often resulted in its destruction. Aroused by curiosity, many easterners joined railroad-sponsored "hunting excursions" into the middle of bison territory where the hunters shot and killed unlimited numbers of bison while remaining protected within their passenger cars.

Paradoxically, by the end of the nineteenth century, it was the scarcity of bison that caused Americans from all sections of the country to look upon the animal as a novelty. As the basis for the bison's novelty changed, so did man's reaction to, and utilization of, bison. By augmenting conservation and economic incentives, novelty has had an indirect influence on the increasing bison population of the twentieth century.

The national parks, wildlife refuges, and game preserves created during the conservation movement of the 1870's through 1910 provide designated areas where contemporary Americans can satisfy their curiosity in bison by passive observation.

Many zoos display bison to aid conservation as well as to share bison with the general public and particularly with inhabitants of urban areas. Some of the most famous zoos possess herds of from nine to 27 bison.[1] The majority of zoos exhibiting bison, however, possess an average of two. More zoos would like to exhibit bison, but find it difficult to locate and pay the high prices asked for well-formed animals. A few private owners exhibit bison occasionally and simultaneously share their knowledge of bison with all who are interested in hope of encouraging more people to take part in conserving bison.

As a novelty, small herds of one to five bison are sometimes used to attract people to otherwise marginal commercial enterprises or ceremonies. Billboards along many western highways call the attention of motorists to roadside areas where bison can be seen . . . adjacent to souvenir shops or restaurants. In recent years, numerous rodeos have increased their attendance by using bison in contests or in displays for people to view upon entering the rodeo grounds. Hackberry Johnson of Austin, Texas, is one of the few bison owners who leases bison to rodeos primarily as attractions. He states that bison draw many spectators to small rodeos which otherwise might be poorly attended. Playing upon both the novelty and symbolic nature of bison, Indians of the Alabama-Coushatta Indian Reservation near Livingston, Texas, annually attract hundreds of visitors with their "Buffalo Ceremony." Indians of the Taos Pueblo in New Mexico perform a similar "Buffalo Ceremony" which likewise attracts numerous tourists. Taking advantage of a unique economic opportunity, Hackberry Johnson has supplied bison for the Inter-Tribal Ceremonial, held in Gallup, New Mexico, for the last six years.

[1] The New York Zoolozical Park, Bronx, New York, which once possessed the largest confined herd of bison, now possesses only nine bison. The Kansas City Zoo, the second largest zoo in the United States, has a bison herd of 13 animals. The August A. Busch, Jr., Zoological Gardens, St. Louis, Missouri, has the largest private zoological park with the largest zoological herd of 27 bison.

In part, the success of the contemporary bison market can be attributed to the animal's novelty and its symbolic connection with American history. The many conservation and economic-oriented uses of live bison enhance the competitive nature of the market for bison. Commercial outlets for bison meat quickly sell their product by advertising it as a novelty item of limited supply. Patrons are willing to pay relatively high prices for the privilege of buying bison meat merely for personal satisfaction or for the prestige that eating or serving bison meat commands. Tommy Harris, operator of Tommy's Joynt (sic) in San Francisco, sells bison stew daily. He states that: "Tourists are attracted to it [bison stew] because it has so much romance . . . and gives them a feeling of going back in history." Finally, it would indeed be difficult to sell the hide, head, horns, or feet of slaughtered bison if it were not for the novelty of these items.

At least 53 percent of the present bison population exists as an indirect result of novelty. As a stimulus for further increasing the bison population, however, novelty could be a self-defeating process. Should novelty continue to stimulate the bison population, bison could become so common and familiar that owners of small herds could no longer use bison to attract buyers or spectators; bison meat could conceiveably compete with beef in the commercial food market because of inevitably lower prices; and a market for bison heads, horns, hides, and feet would probably be non-existent. Nevertheless, it appears that novelty will continue to stimulate a greater bison population until the bison is no longer novel.

Strong young buffalo bull portrait which illustrates the massive head and compact snout which serves the buffalo well for winter grazing under the cold northern snows.

Chapter Six

The Bison: Research

Although literate men have lived in proximity with the American bison since about 1600, little scientific investigation has been done to determine and utilize the unique characteristics of this animal. The bison's physical characteristics were the first to attract man's attention. By nature, the bison is unpredictable and intractable. However, man valued the bison as a hardy, meat-producing animal. Thus, the first recorded use of bison for research concerned experimental hybridization intended to reduce the bison's undesireable characteristics while maintaining the desireable ones.

The Bison in Hybridization

As early as 1815, Robert Wickliffe of Kentucky crossbred bison and domestic stock in formal experiments. His intent was to develop a powerful work animal with the strength of bison and the temperament of domestic cattle. Wickliffe attempted to breed a domestic bull to a bison cow. The domestic bull was unwilling to provide service for the cow; however, a bison bull did breed a domestic cow and successfully produced a first generation hybrid. First generation hybrid cows were productive when mated to either a bison or domestic bull, but, according to Wickliffe, the experiments "...have not satisfied me that the half-buffalo will produce again."

Several other early bison raisers hybridized bison and domestic cattle in an attempt to alter the bison's unpredictable temperament. It was also hoped that the hybrid would yield greater quantities of edible meat than either pure-blood bison or domestic cattle. Typical of these experiments were those conducted by Charles J. Jones and Charles Goodnight.

Jones began systematically hybridizing bison with domestic cattle around 1884. Neither domestic cow abortions or death, nor sterility in hybrid males was overcome when domestic cows were crossed with bison bulls. It can be assumed, however, that Jones' experiments were at least partially successful, for numerous hybrids were in his private herd when it was sold at the time of Jones's death in 1913.

Goodnight began similar experiments also about 1884. He sought to develop a healthy, fertile hybrid from a bison bull and domestic cow. By 1917, Goodnight had developed a herd of 40 hybrids which, in his opinion, were far superior to any breed of cattle known. Yet, Goodnight failed to overcome the problems of sterility of male hybrids, and the high rate of cow and calf mortality when bison bulls were mated with domestic cows.

The most significant systematic study of hybridization, using bison, was conducted by the Canadian government between 1916 and 1964. The study was based on the hypothesis that it is possible to develop a herd of hybrid animals that can be economically productive in the northern areas of the Prairie Provinces of Canada.[1] The emphasis of the Wainwright and Manyberries experiments, as the study has become known, was to assess: 1. the thriftiness and hardiness of the bison by domestic crosses; 2. the possibilities of establishing a hybrid herd consistent with the ability of the bison to withstand low

---

[1] The initial experiments were conducted at the Dominion Experimental Station, Scott, Saskatchewan, but were later moved to an enclosure within the Buffalo Park near Wainwright, Alberta. In 1950, the experimental herd was, again, moved to the Dominion Experiment Station at Manyberries, Alberta.

temperatures and the unfavorable weather conditions that drastically affect the productivity of present breeds of domestic cattle; 3. the comparative development, rate of maturity, and beef-producing qualities of hybrid and domestic animals; and 4. problems of male sterility among hybrid animals.

Wainwright and Manyberries Experiments

Elementary problems and rates of reproduction in hybridization were the first topics of intensive study. Between 1916 and 1935, crosses involving bison and domestic bulls resulted in 82 pregnancies with 19 male and 17 female calves being born alive, or a 58 percent rate of successful births. Twenty of the 82 impregnated dams died as a consequence of pregnancy. There were 14 still births, or 22 percent of the total pregnancies, and 12 abortions, or 19.6 percent of the total pregnancies. Many calves were lost in the bison-domestic cow cross because excessive amounts of amniotic fluid, or hydraminos, were formed in the fetal membranes. This did not occur with the domestic bull-bison cow cross.

The rate of mortality among pregnant dams varied significantly, depending on the direction of the cross. Of the 62 successful pregnancies, 15 were sired by domestic bulls and bison dams. Of this cross pattern, 14 calves were born alive, there was one still birth, and no dams died. Of the 26 pregnancies sired by bison bulls and domestic dams, six calves were born alive, there were 11 abortions, and 16 dams died (see Table 10, page 98).

In 1921, yak were added to the experimental herd to aid in producing fertile hybrid males. When crossed with yak hybrids, domestic bulls sired a higher percentage of normal calves than did the reverse cross. There were only six pregnancies between bison bulls and yak or yak hybrid dams, three of which produced live calves. Crossing a bison bull and yak cow appeared to yield higher rates of reproduction and lower rates of mortality than the bison and domestic cross (see Table 11, page 98). However, the yak hybrids did not

TABLE 10 — Breeding Results from Bison by Domestic Crosses at Wainwright from 1916-1935[a]

Sire	Dam	A	B	C	Live Calves	
					Males	Females
Domestic	Bison	*	1	*	7	7
Domestic	½ bison, ½ domestic	1	*	1	7	3
Domestic	¼ bison, ¾ domestic	*	*	*	1	1
Bison	Domestic	11	9	16	2	4
Bison	½ bison, ½ domestic	*	3	2	1	1
Bison	¾ bison, ¼ domestic	*	1	1	1	1
		12	14	20	19	17

[a] After Deakin, Muir and Smith, 1935, p. 20

A—Abortions; B—Still Births; C—Cows that died; *—No occurrence

TABLE 11 — Breeding Results from Yak by Bison Crosses at Wainwright from 1921-1935[a]

Sire	Dam	A	B	C	Live Calves	
					Males	Females
Domestic	Yak	*	*	*	1	1
Domestic	½ yak, ½ domestic	2	1	*	10	3
Domestic	½ yak, ½ bison	*	*	*	2	2
Domestic	½ domestic, ¼ yak, ¼ bison	*	1	*	2	*
Bison	½ yak, ½ domestic	2	1	1	*	2
Yak	domestic	3	2	1	3	8
Yak	bison	*	*	*	*	1
Yak	½ yak, ½ domestic	*	*	1	1	*
Yak	½ bison, ½ domestic	*	*	*	2	1
½ Yak, ½ Domestic	½ yak, ½ domestic	*	1	*	*	*
Total		7	6	3	21	18

[a] After Deakin, Muir and Smith, 1935, p. 20

A—Abortions; B—Still Births; C—Cows that died; *—No occurrence

TABLE 12 — Breeding Results for the Period 1935-1941 at Wainwright, Alberta[a]

Sires	Dams	No.	Breeding	Year Birth	Progeny			
					Live Male	Calves Female	Calf Males	Mortality Females
Angus	bison	9	Hybrids	1935	*	1	*	*
Angus	bison	14	Hybrids	1936	1	2	*	1
Angus & Hereford	bison	71	Hybrids	1937	11	14	*	*
Angus & Hereford	bison	71	Hybrids	1938	12	17	1	§
Angus & Hereford	bison	71	Hybrids	1939	11	15	*	1
Totals					35	49	1	2
Shorthorn & Hereford	hybrids	8	¾ dom.	1935	1	2	*	*
Shorthorn & Hereford	hybrids	9	¾ dom.	1936	*	4	1	*
Hereford	hybrids	13	¾ dom.	1937	3	1	*	*
Hereford	hybrids	13	¾ dom.	1938	3	3	*	*
Angus & Hereford	hybrids	27	¾ dom.	1939	2	9	2	1
Hereford	hybrids	43	¾ dom.	1940	6	15	3	3
Hereford	hybrids	46	¾ dom.	1941	15	13	4	*
Totals					30	47	10	4
Hereford	¾ dom.	2	⅞ dom.	1935	*	*	*	*
Hereford	¾ dom.	2	⅞ dom.	1936	*	*	*	*
Hereford	¾ dom.	7	⅞ dom.	1937	1	*	*	*
Hereford	¾ dom.	7	⅞ dom.	1938	2	3	1	*
Hereford	¾ dom.	8	⅞ dom.	1939	2	1	1	*
Hereford	¾ dom.	11	⅞ dom.	1940	2	3	1	*
31/32 Dom.	¾ dom.	18	55/64 dom.	1941	4	8	3	2
Totals					11	15	6	2
Hereford	⅞ dom.	2	15/16 dom.	1935	*	*	*	§
Hereford	⅞ dom.	2	15/16 dom.	1936	1	*	*	*
Hereford	⅞ dom.	2	15/16 dom.	1937	*	*	*	*
Hereford	⅞ dom.	2	15/16 dom.	1938	*	1	*	*
Hereford	⅞ dom.	2	15/16 dom.	1939	1	*	*	*
Hereford	⅞ dom.	4	15/16 dom.	1940	*	*	*	*
31/32 Dom.	⅞ dom.	5	59/64 dom.	1941	1	3	*	*
Totals					3	4	*	*

*—No Occurrence   §—Abortions   [a] Deakin, *et. al.*, 1943, p. 4

TABLE 13 — Breeding Results, 1937-1947 inclusive at Wainwright, Alberta[a]

Matings Percent Domestic Blood		Number of Matings	No. Live Offspring Born		Offspring Percent Domestic Blood
Sires	Dams		Males	Females	
100	100	213	34	46	50
100	50	250	53	98	75
100	75	79	23	38	87
100	86	37	18	14	93
100	87	22	4	5	94
100	92	7	1	2	96
97	50	271	75	124	73
97	74	107	34	45	86
97	87	5	1	3	92
87	86	5	*	3	87
86	75	73	15	41	80
86	86	74	28	35	86
86	93	3	1	1	89
75	75	32	2	4	75
75	80	4	*	1	78
75	86	20	6	6	80

*—No Occurrence   [a] Logan and Sylvestre, 1950, p. 3

exhibit the desired value as meat-producing animals in North America and were, therefore, eliminated from the experiments after 1928.

This sequence of experiments revealed that sterility among hybrid males, mortality and other breeding problems would have to be overcome before a herd of cattalo could be productively and economically feasible. [Note: "Hybrid" and "cattalo" will be used interchangeably to denote the progeny of any cross between a bison and domestic stock or other hybrids.]

The results of the Wainwright experiments between 1935 and 1947 were very similar to those of the previous period.

They are summarized above (see Tables 12 and 13, pages 99 and 100 respectively).

One of the major efforts of the Wainwright-Manyberries experiments was to assess the feasibility for a hybrid animal to forage like its bison parent, particularly through deep snow, and to survive in unfavorable climatic conditions. Stimulus for this project came from the belief that winter feeding costs are lower, and rates of survival higher, for animals that are capable of winter grazing.

A study was made of the foraging performance of different breeds of cattle and cattalo during a given 79-day period. The results revealed that cattalo grazed during a greater number of days than did the domestic cattle, that a greater proportion of all the cattalo went out to graze than was true of domestic cattle, and that on all but five days of the experiment the 39 half-bison cows were usually grazing as a group. Unlike the other breeds of animals involved (Hereford, Shorthorn, Angus, and quarter-bison cattalo), the half-bison were capable of caring for themselves under extremely adverse climatic conditions. Rather than pawing to locate grass, they rooted like pure-blood bison with their muzzles plowing through the snow in search of food. This study tentatively proved that hybrid bison are hardier range animals under adverse climatic conditions than are domestic cattle.

To further test the cattalo's ability to subsist under unfavorable climatic conditions, the differences in natural insulation between various breeds of domestic cattle and the bison hybrid's coat were analyzed. In February of 1952, 1953, and 1959, hair samples were studied from the coats of bison, bison hybrids, and cattle. It was found that the coats of cattle adapt to changing climatic conditions; however, bison and hybrid coats are superior in weight of hair per unit area, due to a greater density of hair. Hair length was very similar among the coats of the various animals, but the fiber of the bison and hybrid was thinner than that of the cattle. The pelage characteristics exhibited by bison and hybrids are valuable as insulators from extreme hot and cold temperatures in areas where extremes of climate prevail. Thus, the hybrid represents a valuable improvement over pure domestic cattle breeds in being able to subsist in unfavorable climatic situations.

Between 1949 and 1950, the observeable differences between hybrid and Hereford calves on similar feedlots were investigated at the Dominion Range Experiment Station, Manyberries, Alberta. Experiment results revealed that Hereford calves made greater and seemingly more efficient feedlot gains than did the hybrids. Yet, on examining the carcasses, it was concluded that there should be no difficulty in marketing hybrid beef even though the carcass grade was generally lower for the hybrid than for the Hereford.[2]

In 1952-53 and 1956-57, additional experiments were conducted to obtain comparative data on the rate and efficiency of gain, carcass grades, dressing percentages, and proportion of carcass weight in the hindquarters of bison, cattalo, and Hereford calves. According to H. F. Peters, superintendent of the Dominion Range Experiment Station, the experiments showed that bison were generally least efficient and Hereford most efficient in total digestible nutrients utilized per pound of gain. Hereford stock proved to be the superior weight gainers, with cattalo second and bison last. The Hereford gained an average of 45 pounds more than the cattalo of backcross and inter-bred cows, 102 pounds more than the cattalo of hybrid cows, and 250 pounds more than the pure-bred bison. There were reductions in carcass grade and the percentage of carcass weight in the hindquarters, and an increase in the dressing percentages as the proportion of bison parentage increased in the animals.[3]

[2] It is difficult to compare the meat producing capacities of buffalo and Hereford because buffalo have never been selectively bred for their meat producing characteristics, while Hereford have been actively bred for their meat producing abilities.

[3] The author takes issue with the manner in which Mr. Peters has manipulated and interpreted his data, especially with regard to the bison's ability to utilize feed in producing meat. See Table 3 and the text page 71.

Cow productivity was still another major area of investigation at Manyberries. Hybrid cows were approximately equal to domestic cattle in fertility when the number of calves each had produced had been adjusted for sex ratio due to the tendency among all hybrid animals to produce female progeny out of proportion to male progeny. The number of calves alive at birth per hundred cows was equal for hybrids and domestic cattle. The size of the calves, irrespective of their sex, was largely a function of their parentage. The higher the percentage of bison blood in the parents, the less the calves weighed at birth. The relatively low weight of many hybrid calves caused numerous calves to die. This congenital condition results from a general incompatibility of the diverse genotypes of the parent species.

The most important consideration given to hybrid studies at Manyberries was the most unimprovable aspect of the hybrid—male sterility. It has been suggested that spermatogenesis might take place at a significantly higher temperature in bison than in domestic cattle, and that the disparity between these temperatures adversely affects spermatogenesis in the hybrid. However, experiments revealed that bison exhibit an intratesticular temperature of 93.9 degrees F., cattalo 86.8 degrees F., and Hereford 91.0 degrees F. This range of temperatures appears safe for the production of active, fertile spermatozoa and does not appear to be the direct cause of male hybrid sterility.

Because intratesticular temperatures appear to be normal in hybrid bison, the hybrids have never been tested as cryptochides which might be a possible reason for sterility. Sterility might also be caused by a mismatch of chromosomes. The chromosomes of bison and domestic cattle are similar in diploid number and gross chromosome structure, differing only in the Y chromosome. Yet, P. K. Basrur, a research scientist, is convinced that a general lack of compatibility of genes exists between the bison and domestic cattle.

Breeding the hybrid male back toward either of its pure lineages statistically raises the fertility rate as the undetermined damages resulting from hybridization are mitigated. When the hybridization process has been carried to the level of 15/16ths domestic or bison, there are occasional signs of fertility. When the hybrid reaches the level of 31/32nds domestic or bison, the bull is usually fertile.

Bison in Hybridization: an Assessment

The favorable assets exhibited by cattalo make the animal appear to be both useful and valuable to man. Cattalo are capable of thriving, without shelter, in regions where the environmental conditions are harmful to domestic breeds of cattle. In winter, cattalo will root through the snow for their forage. During blizzards, the cattalo will face directly into the storm and hold their ground as a herd. In contrast, cattle separate when drifting with a storm and, consequently, are often frozen to death. Cattalo meat production does not appear to be inferior to domestic beef, and many people claim the meats are similar in taste. Finally, hybrid cows are approximately equal to domestic cattle in fertility and should be able to reproduce at a comparable rate.

However, the realities of high calf mortality rates, high rate of dam loss, and, most important, sterility of hybrid males eclipse the favorable assets of the hybrid. Hybrids must be fertile and capable of reproducing at a rate commensurate with the various commercial breeds of domestic cattle if cattalo are to be practical as meat-producers in contemporary North America. Cattalo fail to satisfy this criterion because of male sterility. Thus, the hybridization of bison and domestic cattle has not produced an animal that is more than merely a valuable source of experimentation.

Today the number of bison used in hybridization is minimal. Approximately 3.5 percent of all bison raisers in the United States are actively experimenting with bison-domestic cattle hybridization. Harry Pon of Arcadia, California, is one of several individuals concerned with the hybridization of bison on a commerical basis. Many others are occasional hybridizers of bison and domestic cattle for personal interest. Each hopes to overcome the problem of hybrid sterility in males in order to produce an animal that can become commercially valuable.

The Bison in Contemporary Research

With the exception of the described experiments in hybridization, the value of bison in research ramains relatively unexplored, for few researchers are aware of the qualities of bison that would be worthy of investigation.

Dr. Henry O. Dunn, Senior Research Associate at the New York Veterinary College, believes that cattalo represent a challenging problem in reproductive-genetic studies. However, the problem has not been defined, nor have solutions been sought.

Dr. R. L. Niece, of the Institute of Cancer Research, proposes that the usefulness of bison in medical research lies within three general areas of investigation: 1. the effects of the "genetic bottle-neck" resulting from the rapid reduction of the bison population in the nineteenth century; 2. the determination of amino acid sequences of homologous proteins for information relating to evolutionary and genetic mechanisms; and 3. the hybridization of bison and the hybrid's relationship to currently extinct taxonomic units. Once again, there is no evidence to indicate that these possible areas of investigation have been explored.

Dr. Dwain W. Cummings, chairman of the Research Committee of the National Buffalo Association, believes much necessary and valuable experimentation could be done with the buffalo in a number of areas. One of the most promising areas to date is the investigation of the relationship between the buffalo and various aspects of human disease. Of current interest to Dr. Cummings is the relationship between the buf-

falo's extraordinary resistance to cancer and the apparent resistance to cancer exhibited by people who have eaten bison
meat. However, Dr. Niece, suggests that the immunity of
buffalo to cancer might be real or only apparent due to the
relatively short life span of the animal when compared to the
life span of man, even though bison have been known to live
to the age of 50 years. Whichever is the case, more research
must be done to answer the unknown relationship between
buffalo and cancer. Presently, Dr. Cummings is using buffalo
in the production of antilymphocyte serum which can successfully be used by humans.[4]

Related to human health is the apparent low incidence
of allergic reaction of people to buffalo meat. Proof of this
would allow many food-allergic individuals, who are sensitive
to beef, to include bison meat in their diets. This will satisfy
nutrient requirements which must be otherwise artifically
produced or are deficient in their diets. Presently work is
being done with the buffalo as part of a large-scale research
project which will last for the next five to ten years. Under
the leadership of Dr. Elizabeth Rust of South Dakota State
University, the project, entitled "The Nutritive Value and
Utilization of South Dakota Products," buffalo will be studied
to help better understand the exact qualities of bison meat,
especially in terms of its nutritive characteristics. To date,
Dr. Rust and her colleagues have done only fragmentary and
introductory analyses of bison fat, particularly in terms of
composition. According to Dr. Rust: "The thing that makes
this fat unique is the unusually high percentages of the poly-
unsaturated fatty acids for an animal fat. From a nutritional
standpoint we would consider this fat a very good to excellent
source of the essential fatty acids." Although Dr. Rust's
studies are far from complete, she recognizes that buffalo
meat has some unique characteristics.

[4] At the time of writing the full ramifications and test results of
Dr. Cummings' serum were unavailable, particularly as they related to
human use of the serum in combating disease.

Conclusion

Historically, the bison used in hybridization experiments represented a significant portion of the privately-owned bison population. At present, the precise number of bison involved in formal scientific research is unknown, however, it is undoubtedly very small. The very factors that have favorably influenced the increased bison population, i.e., the limited supply and high cost of bison, have impeded the use of bison in research. Perhaps more important is the general ignorance among researchers regarding the bison's potential in genetic or evolutionary studies, cancer and cholesterol research, or as a meat-producer.

The future of bison in research is a matter of speculation. *If* extensive research were conducted with bison, and if the research revealed new and valuable uses for bison, commercially or otherwise, the bison population might be increased in two ways. First, the number of bison used by researchers would call for an increase in the population to a very limited extent. On the other hand, favorable findings on the bison's potential would presumably increase the demand for bison and encourage more bison raisers to maintain larger herds which could then be sold to a commercially expanding market.

References and Further Readings

Baier, J. G., Jr, and Wolfe, H. R. "Quantitative Serologic Relationships within the Artiodactyia," *Zoologica*, Vol. 27(1), 1942, pp. 17-24.

Basrur, P. K., *et. al.* "Chromosomes of Cattle, Bison and Their Hybrid, the Cattalo," *American Journal of Veterinary Research*, Vol. 28(126), 1967, pp. 1419-1424.

Baughman, J. L. "Climate, Cattle, and Cross-breeding," *Texas Journal of Science*, Vol. 3, 1951, pp. 253-304.

Boyd, M. M. "A Short Account of an Experiment in Crossing the American Bison with Domestic Cattle," *American Breeders' Association Annual Report No. 4*, 1908, pp. 324-331.

————. "Crossing Bison and Cattle," *Journal of Heredity*, Vol. 5, 1914, pp. 189-197.

Braend, M., and Gasparski, J. "Haemoglobin and Transferrin of European Bison and Their Cattle Hybrids," *Nature,* Vol. 217, 1967, pp. 98-99.

Craft, W. A. "The Sex Ratio in Mules and Other Hybrid Mammals," *Quarterly Review of Biology,* Vol. 13, 1938, pp. 19-40.

Evans, L. "Comparison of Fatty Acids from the Lipid Classes of Serum Lipoproteins and Other Lipids in Bison," *Journal of Dairy Sciences,* Vol. 47(1), 1964, pp. 45-53.

Garretson, M. S. "The Catalo," *American Bison Society Report, 1917-18,* 1918, pp. 30-37.

Graham, M. "Experimental Crossing of Buffalo with Domestic Cattle," *Canadian Veterinary Record,* Vol. 4, 1923, pp. 266-268.

Haldane, J. B. S. "Sex Ratio and Unisexual Sterility in Hybrid Animals," *Journal of Genetics,* Vol. 12(2), 1922, pp. 101-109.

Iwanoff, E. "Die Fruchtbarkeit der Hybriden des Bos taurus und des Bison americanus," *Biologisches Zentralblatt,* Bd. 31, 1911, pp. 21-24.

Jones, C. J. "Breeding Catalo," *American Breeders' Association Annual Report No. 3,* 1907, pp. 161-165.

Logan, V. S.; and Sylvestre, P. E. *Hybridization of Domestic Beef Cattle and Buffalo, A Progress Statement, 1950,* Ottawa: Department of Agriculture, Canada, 1950.

Peters, H. F. *Experience with Yak Crosses in Canada, Adapted from Reports of the Wainwright Experiment on Hybridization of Domestic Cattle, American Bison and Yak,* Ottawa: Canadian Department of Agriculture [mimeograph], 1968.

Sylvestre, P. E., Logan, V. S., and Muir, G. W. "Hybridization of Domestic Cattle and Bison," *Canadian Department of Agriculture Report,* 1948.

Wheeler, D. "Oh, They Have a Home Where the Catalo Roam," *The Billings Gazette Sunday Magazine,* (1 December), 1968, p. 15.

Chapter Seven

Epilogue

Throughout its long existence, the American bison has had to make several major transitions in order to survive in an ever changing environment. Some of these transitions have been biological; others, and possibly the most demanding, have been solely in the minds of men.

Biologically it was necessary for the buffalo, especially the Plains-type, to make the transition from a forest browser to plains grazer in order to utilize the abundance of food available on the plains of North America. This early transition left its mark on the buffalo in terms of stature and coloration. Much later, as man rapidly decimated the vast herds of wild bison, new instincts had to be developed that would help protect the buffalo from man. Thus, the once fearless, free-roaming buffalo became wary, nervous, sensitive to man's proximity, and sought protection from man in isolated sanctuaries. This later biological transition came almost too late, for by the time new instinctual patterns had become ingrained in the buffalo, the animal was already an endangered species in the United States.

The transitions the buffalo has had to undergo in the minds of men have been far more subtle than the biological transitions. The first was the decision by man to conserve an overexploited and endangered animal. From earliest recorded

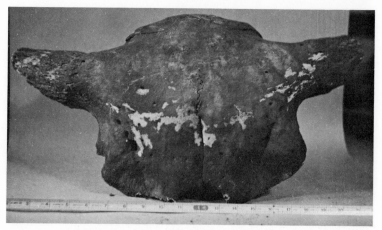

Courtesy Minn. School of Diving

Prehistoric buffalo skull cap and horns found in northern Minnesota lake in summer, 1969. Dating of bones puts age between 10,000 and 12,000 years ago. Large quantity of bones, including human, were found by divers covered by silt and sand in 8 feet of water.

times, but particularly in the nineteenth century, man has exploited the buffalo as a source of food, raw materials, game to be killed for sheer psychological enjoyment, or as an economically valuable commodity. Emotionally man was blinded by the abundance of buffalo on the Great Plains. Many settlers, hunters, and sportsmen were unaware of the magnitude of their killing. Consequently, the nation did not react to the resultant plight of the animal until the 60 million buffalo were nearly exterminated by the unconcerned population of an expanding American civilization.

Slowly, however, people became aware of the slaughter of buffalo on the western Plains. Private citizens responded to the crisis by writing emotionally charged pleas for the public to change its attitudes and actions toward the bison, e.g., "Working to Save the Bison," "Last Effort to Save the Bison." Although the writers successfully stimulated the conservation of the buffalo, the inaccuracies and incongruities pervading their literature placed the bison in an unrealistic sentimental position which has become commonly accepted as the

Courtesy Minn. School of Diving

Prehistoric dorsal vertebrae found with skull on page 110. From the size of this vertebrae, and skull, the buffalo must have been almost half again the size of present day buffalo.

status quo of the buffalo in contemporary literature and thought. This static representation of the buffalo has caused the animal to be regarded almost exclusively as a symbol of American heritage. As a consequence of this all pervasive attitude, the majority of Americans complaisantly believe that buffalo have been consigned to a limited number of parks and zoos, road-side attractions, and rodeo grounds, so that contemporary and

SERVING
BUFFALO
CAN BE FUN!

COCKTAIL BUFFALO MEAT BALLS
IN TOMATO-WINE SAUCE

1 lb. buffalo burger	1 tbsp. Worcestershire Sauce
¼ lb. pork (finely ground)	1 chicken bouillon cube
1 small onion	¼ tsp. salt
1 small clove garlic (minced)	1 cup water
1 small egg	2 tbsp. tomato puree, or to taste
1 tsp. parsley (finely chopped)	1 cup olive oil
1 tsp. lemon juice	1 cup white wine

In mixing bowl combine the meats, onion, garlic, egg, lemon juice, Worcestershire Sauce, parsley and salt.

Knead the mixture very well and roll into small meat balls. Heat olive oil over medium heat until very hot and fry meat balls until brown on all sides.

In sauce pan over low heat dissolve bouillon in 1 cup of water. Slowly add tomato puree and wine. Let mixture come to a boil. Then pour over meat balls, cover and simmer fifteen minutes.

If prepared in advance, reheat before placing in chafing dish to serve.

Red Owl Stores, Inc.

Example of promotional leaflet distributed by a midwestern chain store to encourage the purchase and use of buffalo meat.

future generations can *observe* the beast. Little else is known or appreciated about the buffalo by the general public.

Included in the transition of buffalo in the minds of men has been the change in attitude toward the economic utilization of bison. In the early decades of the nineteenth century, the greatest value of the buffalo, commercially and otherwise, was in the animal's meat. However, later in the 1800's, the value of the bison was in the animal's hide, with very little atten- tion given to the utilization of the meat. Meat was left to rot on the plains either for the sake of expediency in obtaining hides or because so many buffalo were being slaughtered an- nually that the buffalo meat market was grossly over-supplied. Consequently, the value of the buffalo's hide alone stimulated the prodigious slaughter, which left fewer than 20 wild buffalo in the United States.

In the twentieth century the characteristics of the buffalo's value changed once again. No longer were there vast, seemingly unlimited supplies of buffalo. With few wild buffalo avail- able, waste and uncontrolled killing were no longer tolerated. No longer could the full value of the bison be measured by one single part of the animal, i.e., the hide or meat. As a consequence, today there is a very lucrative market for live bison and all its products.

A third transition is still taking place. This final transi- tion is concerned with the objective, analytical investigations involving buffalo. The emotionalism generated by the very mention of buffalo has long obscured the true status and relevancy of the animal in modern America. Much research work has been done to shed new light on the bison and its true place in history. However, few people are aware of the characteristics of the buffalo as an animal of contemporary America. This tends to further restrict the potential of the bison/bison product market. Consequently, the bison product market is extremely expensive to operate and is far from being fully developed. These limitations retard the growth of the American buffalo population which then reinforces the already over-played novelty aspect of the buffalo and allows the perpetuation of its use as a symbol. Objective research on the physical characteristics of bison could be one of the most influential factors in altering this situation. If the reali- ties of such matters as the relationship between bison and cancer, nutritional characteristics of buffalo meat, broad comparative-development studies of buffalo and cattle, and possible plasma synthesis for human use could be made universal, new public interest could stimulate still another attitude change toward the bison and its place in modern, twentieth century America.

This book has attempted to give a new perspective on the problems and potentials of buffalo management in contemporary America. Any study undertaken to help understand the buffalo in twentieth century America is complicated by the many factors working cooperatively to produce any given phenomonon, e.g., the impact of conservationalism, novelty, and emotionalism on an increasing buffalo population. Each in its own way affects the rate of increase, but separately they are less effective stimulators.

It seems that the current sentimental status of buffalo will be little changed until the bison passes entirely through the third transition—objectivity—which will then permit man to focus on the animal's potential value rather than its emotional appeal. To accomplish this, accurate, objective information, based on scientific research, must be disseminated to make all aspects of the buffalo familiar to the general public. Only then will people realize that, with a population of over 17,000 buffalo in the United States, the productive utilization of buffalo, rather than conservation, is now the challenge.

APPENDIX A:

The Questionnaires Used

Much of the information presented in this book was collected through response to two questionnaires.

Questionnaire Form 1 was a self-addressed postal card. The cards were mailed to persons and agencies known to have owned buffalo in the United States as of 1964, as recorded in the U. S. Department of Agriculture files. Since 1964 the Department of Agriculture has made only minimal efforts to update their listing of buffalo raisers. Consequently, their files were outdated. Respondents were requested to state their names, current addresses, number of buffalo owned, and the names of any individual(s) who, to the knowledge of the respondent, had begun raising buffalo after 1964. This questionnaire was sent out to accomplish two purposes. The first was to update the Department of Agriculture's bison-owner list; and secondly, to establish an accurate census of the bison in the United States.

Respondents to Questionnaire Form 2 were randomly selected from the known bison raisers in the United States. Eight general questions were directed toward the possible reasons for the restoration of buffalo, problems encountered with ownership of buffalo, and the questionnaire also allowed latitude for personal expression on the part of each respondent.

The number of returns from Questionnaire Form 1 was remarkably high. Of the 712 postal cards mailed to buffalo raisers, approximately 585 cards were returned to the author with complete information. This represented an 82.3 percent rate of compliance.

There were fewer returns from Questionnaire Form 2; because the questionnaire form was long and required concerted time and effort to complete it. Consequently, fewer people were willing to complete this questionnaire. On the presumption that the majority of zoos would elicit similar

responses to the eight questions, many of the zoos were eliminated from the mailing of the Questionnaire Form 2. Of the
350 questionnaires mailed, only 133 were returned, repre-
senting a 38 percent compliance.

The Results

Responses to Questionnaire Form 1 indicate that there
are approximately 354 persons actively raising bison in the
United States. An additional 75 buffalo raisers were accounted
for through lists obtained from individual states, and 35 persons known to possess bison, but who failed to respond to the
questionnaire. Each of these 35 persons has been given a
maximum of one buffalo to be included in the total bison
population, however, even this number may not accurately
reflect the buffalo they own, for they presumably own many
more. Through this method, there were 464 bison raisers, including private citizens, national and state parks, and zoos,
who owned well over 17,000 buffalo. The average number
of bison owned per person or agency was approximately 37.
Only 40 respondents raised more buffalo than the average,
however, these respondents accounted for approximately 12,687
bison, and only 10 respondents owned 8,987, or over half the
total bison population as established by the census.

The buffalo population as suggested by this study (more
than 17,000) is greater than estimates thus far suggested by
the various state and national government agencies for the
United States. These agencies have estimated that there are
roughly 20,000 to 22,000 buffalo in the United States and
Canada combined. However, the number of bison in Wood
Buffalo National Park, Alberta, Canada, alone is estimated to
be more than 10,000 but less than 16,000 animals. A more
accurate estimate of the number of buffalo in the United States
and Canada would be in excess of 35,000 to 40,000. This
figure takes into consideration the fact that not all buffalo
raisers in the United States were contacted, and many of those
originally contacted during this study did not respond. Con-

sequently, 35,000 to 40,000 buffalo might be far too low an estimate in terms of the actual number of bison in North America today.

The responses to Questionnaire Form 2 have been tabulated below. The responses and number of buffalo for each question were considered independently of the other seven questions. The percentages were derived in the following manner: 1. similar responses to a given question were grouped together and computed against the total number of responses in terms of percentages; and 2. the total number of bison owned by each respondent was considered in each response given by the respondent to each question. The total number of buffalo involved in each group of similar responses was added and computed as percentages. Thus, the percentages for each question were not computed on an equal number of total responses or buffalo owned, for often the respondents would leave a particular question unanswered, or would answer one question in such a manner as to necessitate the answer being placed within more than one category for responses to the same question.

Responses to Question One:

Why did the respondent originally invest in bison?

Total responses — 142

Represents an overall total of 11,193 bison in sample.

	Responses	Bison
1. For Attractions:		
Parks, Refuges and State		
Depts. of conservation	41 - 28.9%	5010 - 44.8%
Zoos	13 - 9.2%	78 - 0.7%
For use in Rodeos	1 - 0.7%	2 - 0.01%
For use in Indian		
Ceremonials	1 - 0.7%	n.d.
Total for Attractions	56 - 39.5%	5090 - 45.5%
2. For use in hybridization ..	5 - 3.5%	64 - 0.6%

3. Income from sale of bison
   or meat ....   24 - 16.9%   4497 - 40.2%
4. Hobby from novelty or
   unusualness of the animal
   and personal interest ...   44 - 31.0%   685 - 6.0%
5. Symbolism ....   10 - 7.0%   265 - 2.6%
6. Others ....   3 - 2.1%   248 - 2.2%

Responses to Question Two:

Had the respondent noticed any change in the bison's temperament?

Total Responses — 165
Represents an overall total of 10,959 bison in sample.

	Responses	Bison
1. No Change	61 - 37.4%	3520 - 32.1%
2. Tamer, calmer	32 - 19.3%	2304 - 21.0%
3. More nervous	19 - 11.5%	105 - 0.9%
4. Unpredictable	9 - 5.5%	2233 - 20.4%
5. Trainable	7 - 4.2%	584 - 5.3%
6. Equal to cattle	5 - 3.0%	66 - 0.6%
7. More aggressive with increased age	5 - 3.0%	41 - 0.4%
8. Stronger	5 - 3.0%	274 - 2.5%
9. Wilder	3 - 1.8%	132 - 1.2%
10. Changes with various feeds	3 - 1.8%	11 - 0.1%
11. Males aggressive toward calves	2 - 1.2%	5 - 0.05%
12. Meaner	2 - 1.2%	3 - 0.03%
13. Diminution of size, result of in-breeding	1 - 0.6%	21 - 0.2%

Responses to Question Three:

What problems have there been with the raising of bison?

Total Responses — 144

Represents an overall total of 9,228 bison in sample.

		Responses	Bison
1.	No problems	59 - 40.9%	821 - 8.9%
2.	Internal parasites	18 - 12.5%	457 - 4.9%
3.	Brucellosis	12 - 8.3%	4197 - 45.5%
4.	Food problems	11 - 7.6%	2359 - 25.6%
5.	Low rates of reproduction	11 - 7.6%	451 - 5.0%
6.	Sterility	10 - 7.0%	148 - 1.6%
7.	Won't feed with domestic cattle	9 - 4.2%	97 - 1.0%
8.	Other diseases, e.g., Pink eye	5 - 3.5%	58 - 0.6%
9.	Adults dangerous to calves	2 - 1.4%	5 - 0.05%
10.	In-breeding	1 - 0.6%	214 - 2.3%
11.	*Leptospirosis pomona* and *Pasterella multococida*	*	329 - 3.6%
12.	Low titrations	*	32 - 0.4%
13.	"Scours"	*	20 - 0.2%
14.	Herd *TOO* prolific	*	13 - 0.2%
15.	External parasites	*	10 - 0.1%
16.	Disposing of extra bulls	*	9 - 0.1%
17.	Miscellaneous other problems	3 - 1.8%	8 - 0.1%

*—Indicates only one response and 0.6 percent of total each.

Responses to Question Four:

Has the respondent attempted any selective breeding?

Total Responses — 126

Represents an overall total of 10,365 bison in sample.

		Responses	Bison
1.	Do not practice any type of selective breeding	95 - 75.4%	1772 - 17.1%

2. Do practice various types of
   selective breeding ......   31 - 24.6%   8593 - 82.9%
Types of selective breeding:
For good looks ....   8 - 6.4%   2713 - 26.2%
For hardier, larger animals ....   7 - 5.6%   5368 - 51.8%
For use in cross-breeding .....   7 - 5.6%   379 - 3.6%
Selective breeding: unspecific ..   5 - 4.0%   72 - 0.7%
Elimination of shy,
   non-breeding cows ....   2 - 1.6%   34 - 0.3%
Prevention of inbreeding .....   1 - 0.8%   12 - 0.1%

Responses to Question Five:

Do the respondents have any plans to increase the size
of their herd?

Total Responses — 137
Represents a total of 10,141 bison in sample.

	Responses	Bison
1. Plan to increase the size of their herds	79 - 57.6%	5559 - 54.8%
Methods of increasing herd size:		
By natural increase	63 - 45.9%	3859 - 38.1%
By purchase	16 - 11.7%	1700 - 16.8%
2. No plans to increase herd size	58 - 42.3%	4582 - 45.2%

Responses to Question Six:

Has bison raising met the respondent's expectations?

Total Responses — 135
Represents an overall total of 15,598 bison in sample.

	Responses	Bison
1. Yes	106 - 88.2%	15,342 - 98.4%
Why raising has met expectations:		
Novelty/drawing attraction	21 - 19.8%	2,067 - 13.4%
Pleasure	13 - 12.3%	119 - 0.8%

Public is enjoying the

animals ....   10 - 9.4%   2,200 - 14.4%

Good price for meat .....   9 - 8.5%   2,280 - 14.8%

Self-sustaining ....   6 - 5.6%   2,280 - 14.8%

Conserve bison ....   6 - 5.6%   1,977 - 12.8%

Offers a chance for study .   5 - 4.7%   1,061 - 6.9%

Very prolific ....   1 - 0.9%   10 - 0.1%

Hardy and healthy ......   1 - 0.9%   9 - 0.1%

2. No ....   29 - 11.8%   256 - 1.7%

Responses to Question Seven:

Is the raising of bison a prosperous undertaking?

Total Responses — 128

Represents an overall total of 12,307 bison in sample.

	Responses	Bison
1. Yes	105 - 82.0%	11,795 - 95.8%

Reasons:

Easy to sell meat,

new markets   37

Large demand for live

animals   12

For tourists   9

Novelty   8

Demand for hides   4

Can outproduce cattle

in meat   2

| 2. No .... | 23 - 17.9% | 512 - 4.2% |

Reasons:

Won't compete with beef   4

Takes a particular type

of handling; know-how   4

Gestation period too long   3

Difficult to find a market   3

Not economical on

small scale   2

3. Yes, but ....   5 - 4.8%   1,284 - 10.9%
Reasons:
    Overproduction might hurt
      prices   2
    Will not go beyond
      novelty food stage ...   1
    Transportation costs high .   1
    Government rules
      becoming too strict ...   1

Responses to Question Eight:

Are there different ends for raising bison across the country?

Total Responses — 43
Represents an overall total of 4,027 bison in sample.

	Responses	Bison
1. Yes	35 - 81.4%	2007 - 49.8%
2. No	8 - 18.6%	2020 - 50.2%

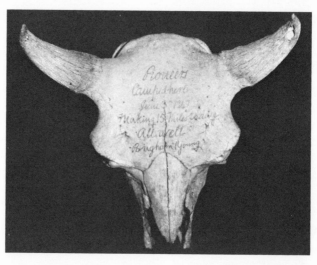

A Mormon sign-post. The legend on the skull reads, "Pioneers camped here, June 3, 1847. Making 15 miles today — All well — Brigham Young."

APPENDIX B:

The Indian, the Horse, and the Buffalo

When most Americans imagine the North American Indian, they visualize a Plains Indian. Few people are familiar with the bean, squash, and corn cultivator of the eastern woodlands. The common representation of an Indian is one in which a warrior is dressed in buckskins, leggings, beads, a bone breastplate, and a war bonnet made of eagle feathers, and riding a semi-tamed mustang. This image of the Indian would have been entirely different had it not been for the reintroduction of the horse to North America by the Spanish in the 1500's.

Prior to the return of the horse to the plains of North America, most of the Indians recognized by name today were subsistence hunters and gatherers, or marginal subsistence farmers of the woodlands bordering the Great Plains. The plains then represented many threats to the pedestrian Indian whose mobility was extremely limited. Threat of death was constant for a wind-driven grass fire or stampeding herd of wild buffalo could easily overtake a man on foot. Further, the plains held few items the Indians could easily obtain or use. This included the rich soil of the plains, for the sod was too thick and tough to be broken by the Indian's primitive hand-tools such as the dibble stick. Consequently, the Indian seldom ventured far into the plains and, therefore, had only limited, seasonal contact with buffalo when the animals migrated near to Indian villages.

With the coming of the horse, the Indian's fears of the Great Plains, grass fires, and buffalo changed. Although the Indian initially hunted horses just as he did any other large game, he soon learned the usefulness of the horse as something other than a source of food. Of greatest importance was the increased mobility provided by the horse. Soon the Indian began trading or stealing horses. Realizing that the horse meant independence, the Spanish would not enter into

Northern Cheyenne women dressing buffalo hides. This 1878 photograph
shows the hides staked; the meat drying on racks in the background
near the tipis.

horse-trading with the Indians. However, Indians, who worked
for the Spanish as cattle or horse herders, often stole entire
herds of both cattle and horses. In addition, horse-trading was
carried on between Indian tribes. Thus, the horse rapidly
proliferated throughout the tribes bordering on the Great Plains.

Indian tribes from all over the country were drawn to
the plains by the promise of new wealth measured in terms
of plentiful food supplies. Now the Indian had the means

by which to utilize the unending herds of buffalo as a constant source of food. Soon the Blackfoot, Crow, Dakota (Sioux), Ute, Comanche, Pawnee, Cheyenne, Kiowa tribes left their subsistence agriculture to tap the wealth of the Great Plains by adopting a life of nomadic hunting. Thus began what has become known as the Horse Culture Period in the history of the North American Indian (1540-1880).

In order to adapt to life on the plains, the Indian's culture had to change. A changed value system had to consider the benefits derived from using the horse. Prestige was gained by being a warrior and good horseman. No longer was age the sole criterion for leadership. New social systems developed to accommodate the constant movement of tribes. New weapons were developed for use on horseback. The long bow, so useful in forests, was replaced by a much shorter, stronger bow which could be easily loosed from a running horse. If guns were available, only short muskets were accepted, for the long rifle was too unwieldly. Finally, the lance became a major part of the Indian's arsenal for use against both enemies and the buffalo.

Buffalo provided nearly everything the Indian needed to survive in relative comfort on the plains. Prepared buffalo hides quickly replaced the strips of birchbark previously used to cover tipis, or in place of earth lodges. Hides made the tipis considerably larger, lighter, and more portable. Buffalo hides also provided other useful materials. From the thicker, tougher bull's hide came material for shields that could deflect arrows or even a musket ball. Small round-bottom boats were made from "green" hides. Clothing was made from the less tough hides. Leftover strips of hide went into the making of ropes. Hides with hair remaining were used as blankets and coats during the winter. The hair, itself, was woven to make belts, garters, and light summer blankets. The horns were used to make cups, bows, and other utensils. The sinew provided crude thread for sewing. The bladder and stomach provided waterproof containers. And the vital organs, along with the meat which was prepared in a variety of ways, provided the bulk of the Indians' diet. Even the ribs of the buffalo were used as runners for small sleds, and the hooves were made into glue for use in the preparation of the war bonnet. Finally, buffalo dung provided fuel for the camp and cooking fires on the treeless plains.

When the white man began settling in the western United States, his occupation of the Great Plains was retarded by the Indian. The Indians then represented a mighty and well-adapted fighting force. With their horses, bows and arrows, muskets, shields, and the buffalo as a constant source of food, they were almost undefeatable. Unlike the sedentary Indians of the East and South, the Plains Indians were difficult to defeat, for they had no homes to destroy, and they could not easily be attacked because of their mobility. However, as a consequence of the Indians' dependence on the buffalo, the decimation of the buffalo meant disaster for the Plains Indians; they had become over-specialized in their way of life and could not adapt to the new West of the white man. As a result, Columbus Delano's wish for the extermination of the buffalo nearly came true, and the Indian was finally pacified.

Artist Frederick Remington's engraving of the Indian Buffalo Dance, shows the intense invocation to the Buffalo Spirit for the return of the great herds of buffalo to the plains.

APPENDIX C:

The American Bison Society and Others

The American Bison Society (ABS) was founded in 1905. Influential persons interested in preserving the buffalo were invited to the first organizational meeting, held at the New York Zoological Park, by Dr. William T. Hornaday. The charter members present that day in the Lion House of the zoo were: Franklin Hooper, William T. Hornaday, A. A. Anderson, Earnest H. Baynes, Edward Cave, Frederic H. Kennard, Francis Piper and Mrs. Piper, Harry V. Radford, Martin Schenck, G. O. Shields, Edmund Seymour, Martin S. Garretson, C. H. Stonebridge, Robert C. Auld, and Charles H. Townsend.

Article II of the Society's constitution states: "The objects of this society shall be the permanent preservation and increase of the American bison." In carrying out this aspect of their charge, the Society became the leading and most effective organization in the United States seeking legislation to preserve the bison as a wild game animal.

When the Society was formed in 1905, according to Garreston in his book *The American Bison*, there were only two herds of buffalo under government supervision. One herd was in the National Zoological Park in Washington, D.C., and the other herd, established in 1903, in the Yellowstone National Park. In 1905, these two herds totaled only twenty-nine bison.

By 1908 the ABS had developed from its original membership of sixteen to a large organization of over 825 members from all segments of American life. By the late 1930's the Society had achieved its objectives, and, therefore, membership began to dwindle. By the late 1950's, the Society was disbanded forever.

In 1964, the complete records of the now historical ABS were sent to the Conservation Section, Denver Public Library, Denver, Colorado, where they are available to any authorized researcher with considerable influence and patience. The amount of information contained in the ABS's files is great. There is information, in fact, the bulk of it, on the attempts made by its membership to stimulate legislation and appropriation of funds for the preservation and maintainence of buffalo in national parks and refuges. For any researcher, this information source is surely a must.

In Denver, Colorado on March 11, 1967, eighty dedicated buffalo raisers joined together to form the National Buffalo Association. This new association seems to have developed out of the innate desire on the part of bison raisers to have a group through which they might come together, discuss problems of common interest, ideas, and the possibilities for the perpetuation of the buffalo, for both economic reasons and for "Americana." After the ABS ceased operation, there was no longer an organization available to the interested buffalo raisers. Now there is the National Buffalo Association. Since its first meeting in 1967, the National Buffalo Association's president has been L. R. Houck, Box 995, Pierre, South Dakota.

On November 14, 1968, the articles of incorporation were authorized for the establishment of the newest fraternity of bison raisers, The Buffalo Breeders of America, Inc. The purpose of this new organization is:

1) to propagate the species of the American bison;
2) to preserve the purity of that animal's blood lines;
3) to organize breeders of bison in the United States and dedicate its membership to the preservation and increase of the bison population; and
4) to hold shows, exhibitions, and sales of bison throughout the United States and to do anything to promote the breeding, exhibition, and preservation of the bison in the United States.

At present, the Buffalo Breeders of America, Inc. is under the directorship of O. A. Cargill, Jr., c/o Hales Building, Oklahoma City, Oklahoma, until such time as the first membership meeting is convened.

Anyone interested in joining either of these two organizations is urged to write to the president of the organizations.

BIBLIOGRAPHY

Allen, G. M. "Our Rarer Mammals," *Audubon Magazine*, Vol. 43(2), 1941, pp. 151-160.

Allen, J. A. "The American Bisons, Living and Extinct," *Memoirs of the Geological Survey of Kentucky*, Vol. 1, Part 2, 1876, pp. i-236.

————. "The Northern Range of the Bison," *American Naturalist*, Vol. 9, 1877, p. 624.

————. "Former Range of the Buffalo in Virginia," *New York Evening Post*, (December 10) 1889.

————. "The Fossil Bisons of North America," *American Naturalist*, Vol. 33, 1889, pp. 665-666.

Anderson, R. M. "History, Range, and Home Life of the Northern Bison," *Ecological Monographs*, Vol. 11(4), 1941, pp. 347-412.

Andrews, E. N. "A Buffalo Hunt by Rail," *Kansas Magazine*, Vol. 3(5), 1875, pp. 450-458.

Antonius, O. "Bermerkungen über Bastarde und Bastardnucht," *Biologisches General*, Bd. 9(2), 1933, pp. 39-47.

"A Plumber Rounds up the Buffalo," *American Magazine*, Vol. 149(4), 1950, pp. 106-107.

Ashbrook, F. G. *Butchering, Processing, and Preservation of Meat*, New York: Van Nostrand, 1955.

Ashe, T. *Travels in America, Performed in the Year of 1806*, London: Richard Phillips, 1809.

Audubon, J. J. and Bachman, J. *The Quadrupeds of North America* (3 Vols.) New York: V. G. Audubon, 1854.

Baier, J. G., Jr., and Wolfe, H. R. "Quantitative Serologic Relationships within the Artiodactya," *Zoologica*, Vol. 27(1), 1942, pp. 17-24.

Bailey, V. "Buffalo in Oregon," *Journal of Mammalogy*, Vol. 4(4), 1923, pp. 254-255.

Barnes, R. M. "An Albino Buffalo," *Ooelogist*, Vol. 50(10), 1933, pp. 138-139.

Barnes, W. C. "Great American Bison Preserve: Wichita National Forest," *Travel*, Vol. 49(5), 1927, pp. 16-19.

Bartram, Wm. *Travels of William Bartram*. Ed. by M. Van-Doren, New York: Dover Publications, 1928.

Bartram, Wm. "Travels in Georgia and Florida, in 1773-74," *Transactions*, of the American Philosophical Society, Vol. 33(2), 1943, pp. 117-242 [Son of previous entry].

Bascom, K. F. "Silk Buffalo Robes," *Journal of Heredity*, Vol. 3(4), 1922, p. 263.

Basrur, P. K., et. al. "Chromosomes of Cattle, Bison and Their Hybrid, the Cattalo," *American Journal of Veterinary Research*, Vol. 28(126), 1967, pp. 1419-1424.

Baughman, J. L. "Climate, Cattle, and Cross-breeding," *Texas Journal of Science*, Vol. 3, 1951, pp. 253-304.

Baynes, E. H. "Largest Herd of Bison in the World," *Country California(n)*, Vol. 1, 1905, pp. 262-265.

————. "Help Save the Buffalo," *Woman's Home Companion*, Vol. 32, 1905, pp. 20-21.

————. "In the Name of the American Bison," *Harper's Weekly*, Vol. 50, 1906, pp. 404-406.

————. "Fight to Save the Buffalo," *Country Life*, Vol. 13, 1908, pp. 295-298.

————. "Breeding of a Buffalo Team," *Nature Magazine*, Vol. 3, 1924, pp. 267-270.

Benbrooke, E. A., and Sloss, M. W. *Clinical Parasitology*, 3rd ed. Ames, Iowa: Iowa State University Press, 1961.

Bergstrom, R. C. "Sheep Liver Fluke, Fasciola hepatica L., 1758 from Buffalo, Bison bison (L. 1758) in Western Wyoming," *Journal of Parasitology*, Vol. 53(4), 1967, p. 724.

Biggers, D. H. "Buffalo Butchery in Texas was a National Calamity," *Farm and Ranch*, Vol. 44, 1925, pp. 28-29.

"Bison and Cattle Crossed, Hardy Breed Produced," *Science News Letter*, Vol. 74, 1958, p. 152.

"Bison in Alaska," *Journal of Heredity*, Vol. 20, 1929, p. 324.

"Bison, Mammals of New York Past and Present," *New York Conservation Department Information Leaflet*, 1968.

"Bison Near Extinction," *Science News Letter*, Vol. 53, 1948, p. 75.

"Bison a Reappearing American," *Literary Digest*, Vol. 99, 1928, pp. 70-74.

Boyd, M. F. "The Occurrence of the American Bison in Alabama and Florida," *Science*, Vol. 84(2174), 1936, p. 203.

Boyd, M. M. "A Short Account of an Experiment in Crossing the American Bison with Domestic Cattle," *American Breeders' Association Annual Report No. 4*, 1908, pp. 324-331.

————. "Crossing Bison and Cattle," *Journal of Heredity*, Vol. 5, 1914, pp. 189-197.

Braend, M., and Gasparski, J. "Haemoglobin and Transferrin of European Bison and Their Cattle Hybrids," *Nature*, Vol. 217, 1967, pp. 98-99.

Braend, M., and Starmont, C. "Haemoglobin and Transferrin Types in the American Buffalo," *Nature*, Vol. 197(4870), 1963, pp. 910-911.

Branch, E. D. *The Hunting of the Buffalo*, Lincoln, Nebraska: University of Nebraska Press, 1962.

Brown, B. "Railway Excursion and Buffalo Hunt," *Natural History*, Vol. 49, 1942, p. 245.

Bryan, P. "Man and the American Bison," *National Wildlife*, Vol. 2(1), 1963/1964, pp. 46-49.

"Buffalo," *Science*, Vol. 18, 1931, p. 35.

"Buffalo," *Science News Letter*, Vol. 81, 1962, p. 32.

"Buffalo - Cattle Cross Makes Rugged Hombre," *Farm Journal*, Vol. 78, 1954, p. 50.

"Buuffalo Herds Increase Rapidly," *California Cultivator*, Vol. 56, 1921, p. 53.

"Buffalo Meat on War Menus," *Science Digest*, Vol. 13, 1943, p. 11.

"The Buffalo Monarch of the Plains," *Texas Game and Fish*, Vol. 1(8), 1943, pp. 4;16.

"Buffalo on a Bun: Buffaloburgers," *American Magazine*, Vol. 154, 1952, p. 56.

"Buffalo Wins Fight for Survival," *Austin American Statesman*, (30 August) 1970.

Burback, H. J. "Buffalo on the Public Domain," *Our Public Lands*, Vol. 1, 1951, p. 14.

Bureau of Sport Fisheries and Wildlife, Division of Wildlife Refuges, Leaflets 212, *Buffalo Management;* and 413, *Surplus Animal Disposal on National Wildlife Refuges,* 1965 and 1967.

Bushnell, D. I. "Various Uses of Buffalo Hair by the North American Indians," *American Anthropologist*, Vol. 11(4), 1909, pp. 401-425.

Bylin, J. E. "Some Restaurants Add a Buffalo Bill of Fare and People Eat it up," *The Wall Street Journal*, (4 December) 1968.

Cahalane, V. H. "Restoration of Wild Bison," *Transactions of the North American Wildlife Conference*, Vol. 9, 1944, pp. 135-143.

Cameron, A. E. "Notes on Buffalo: Anatomy, Pathological Conditions, and Parasites," *Veterinary Journal*, Vol. 79, 1923, pp. 331-336.

———. "Some Further Notes on Buffalo," *Veterinary Journal*, Vol. 80, 1924, pp. 413-417.

"Can the Buffalo Come Back?" *Popular Science,* Vol. 123, 1933, p. 35.

Castle, C. S. "Remnant of a Mighty Host," *Overland Quarterly,* Vol. 73, 1919, pp. 202-206.

"Cattalo; Crossbred Buffalo and Domestic Cattle," *Time,* Vol. 47, 1946, p. 39.

"Cattalo Herd Established," *Agriculture Gazette of Canada,* Vol. 3, 1916, pp. 208-210.

Cauley, T. J. "What the Passing of the Buffalo Meant to Texas," *Cattleman,* Vol. 14(7), 1929, pp. 32-33.

Chittenden, H. M. *The American Fur Trade of the Far West,* 3 vols. New York: Harper, 1902.

Christy, M. "The Last of the Buffaloes," *Field,* Vol. 72, 1888, pp. 698-699.

Clark, G. "Modern Bison Herd," *American Cattle Producer,* Vol. 26, 1944, pp. 9-10.

Cole, H. H., Ed. *Introduction to Livestock Production,* San Francisco: W. H. Freeman and Co., 1962.

Collins, H. H. *The Unvanquished Buffalo,* New York: Blue Heron Press, 1952.

Congressional Globe, Washington, D.C.: U.S. Government Printing Office [Bound editions only].

Congressional Record, Washington, D.C.: U.S. Government Printing Office [Bound editions only].

Cook, J. R. *The Border and the Buffalo,* Topeka: Crane and Co., 1907.

Cooper, M. M. *Beef Production,* New York: Thomas Nelson, 1953.

Cotton, E. J. "Hybrids," *Canadian Cattleman,* Vol. 12(4), 1949, pp. 12-13; 36-37.

Cowen, J. L. "Trail of the Hide Hunters," *Outing,* Vol. 59, 1911, pp. 153-159.

Craft, W. A. "The Sex Ratio in Mules and Other Hybrid Mammals," *Quarterly Review of Biology,* Vol. 13, 1938, pp. 19-40.

Craig, V. *The Shaggy Ones,* Helena: Montana Fish and Game Department, 1967.

"Creation of a Blizzard-Proof Quadruped; Hybrid of Cattle and Buffaloes," *Current Opinion,* Vol. 70, 1921, pp. 664-665.

Creech, G. T. "Brucella abortus Infection in Male Bison," *North American Veterinarian,* Vol. 11(1), 1929, pp. 35-36.

Cross, J. M. "Dakotas Conserve Land and Buffaloes," *Farmland,* Vol. 36(6), 1969, p. 1;11.

Davis, T. R. "The Buffalo Range," *Harpers' New Monthly Magazine,* Vol. CCXXIV(38), 1869, pp. 147-163.

Davison, E. J. "Buffaloes of Goodnight Ranch," *Ladies' Home Journal,* Vol. 18, 1901, p. 7.

Deakin, A.; Muir, G. W.; and Smith, A. G. "Hybridization of Domestic Cattle, Bison, and Yak, Report of the Wainwright Experiment," *Publication of the Department of Agriculture, Canada, No. 479,* 1935, 30 pp.

Deakin, A.; Muir, G. W.; Smith, A. G.; and MacClellan, A. S. "Hybridization of Domestic Cattle and Buffalo (Bison americanus), Progress of the Wainwright Experiment, 1935-1941," *Department of Agriculture, Experimental Farms Station Report, Canada,* 1943, 10 pp.

Dehnel, A. "Die ersten Hybriden zwischen Bos taursus dom. L. Male und Bison bonasus (L) Female," *Acta Theriologica,* Vol. 5(3), 1961, pp. 45-50.

Demaray, A. E. "Saving the Buffalo," *Outing,* Vol. 81(2), 1922, pp. 116-117.

Demiaszkiewicz, W. "Die Geburt eines Hybriden von Bison bonasus (L) male und Bos taurus dom. (L) female," *Acta Theriologica,* Vol. 5(4), 1961, pp. 51-56.

Department of Agriculture. *Agricultural Statistics,* Washington, D.C.: U.S. Government Printing Office, 1970.

"Developing a New Breed of Cattle," *Producer,* Vol. 7(10), 1926, pp. 30-31.

Devoe, A. "Days of the Bison," *American Mercury,* Vol. 53, 1941, pp. 747-751.

Dickie, F. "Buffalo Cross-Breeding," *National Stockman and Farmer,* Vol. 47, 1923, p. 286.

Diggins, R. V., and Bundy, C. E. *Beef Production,* Englewood Cliffs, New Jersey: Prentice Hall, 1962.

Dikmans, G. "New Records of Helminth Parasites," *Proceedings of the Helminthal Society of Washington,* Vol. 1(2), 1934, pp. 63-64.

Dimmick, S. R. "The Bison—Vanquished Monarch," *Texas Game and Fish,* Vol. 14(2), 1956, pp. 4-5; 30.

Dodge, R. I. *The Plains of the Great West,* New York: G. P. Putnam's Sons, 1877.

Draper, B. "Where the Buffalo Roamed," *Pacific Discovery,* Vol. 3(2), 1950, pp. 14-27.

Drummond, R. O. and Medley, J. G. "Occurrence of Speleognathus australis Womersley in the Nasal Passages of Bison," *Journal of Parisitology,* Vol. 50(23), 1964, p. 655.

Drury, N. B. "Comeback of the Bison," *Rotarian*, Vol. 69, 1946, pp. 20-22.

Dryden, W. J. "Cattalo [A] New Hardy Breed [of Cattle]," *Montana Farmer-Stockman*, Vol. 34(23), 1947, p. 51.

Duffy, P. "The Buffalo Stages a Comeback," *Outdoor Life*, Vol. 67(5), 1931, p. 15; 71.

Dwight, T. *The Northern Traveller*, New York: J and J Harper, 1830.

Edwards, L. L. "Last Stand of the Bison," *Technical World*, Vol. 19, 1913, pp. 892-893.

Eiseley, L. C. "Folsom Mystery: Solution is Largely Contigent on Solution of Another Mystery," *Scientific American*, Vol. 167, 1942, pp. 260-261.

Eliot, S. "Black Beard—The Bison," *The Detroit News, Sunday News Magazine*, (9 August), 1970, p. 2.

Elrod, M. J. "The Montana National Bison Range," *Journal of Mammalogy*, Vol. 7, 1926, pp. 45-48.

Evans, L. "Comparison of Fatty Acids from the Lipid Classes of Serum Lipoproteins and Other Lipids of Bison," *Journal of Dairy Sciences*, Vol. 47(1), 1964, pp. 45-53.

"Extinction of the Buffalo," *Country California(n)*, Vol. 1, 1905, p. 227.

Fielder, M. "Atomic-Age Buffalo," *American Cattle Producer*, Vol. 36, 1955, pp. 9-10.

Fleming, [H. A.] *Goodnight's American Buffalo Ranch, Goodnight, Texas*, Dallas: Fleming and Co., 1910.

Fremont, J. C. *Report of the Exploring Expedition to the Rocky Mountains, in the year 1842, and to Oregon and California in the years 1843-44*, Washington, D.C.; The Senate of the United States, 1845.

Frick, E. J. "Parasitism in Bison," *Journal of the American Veterinary Medical Association*, Vol. 119(896), 1951, p. 387.

Froman, R. "Buffalo that Refused to Vanish," *Readers' Digest*, Vol. 72, 1958, pp. 195-199.

Fullerton, A. "Buffalo, Lord of the North," *Mentor*, Vol. 13, 1925, pp. 22-26.

————. "Livestock and Meat Up North," *Producer*, Vol. 12, 1930, pp. 5-8.

————. "Will the Cattalo Displace the Buffalo?" *Forest and Outdoors*, Vol. 6(3), 1940, pp. 91-92.

Gabrielson, I. N. *Wildlife Refuges*, New York: Macmillian Co., 1943.

Gage, E. W. "Buffalo Round-up at Wainwright," *Travel*, Vol. 66(2), 1935, pp. 33-34.

Gard, W. "Where Buffalo Roamed," *Progressive Farmer*, Vol. LXVIII(8), 1953, p. 18.

————. "On the Buffalo Range," *Texas Parade*, Vol. 15(6), 1954, pp. 41-43.

————. *The Great Buffalo Hunt*, New York: Knopf, 1959.

Garretson, M. S. "The Catalo," *The American Bison Society Report, 1917-1918*, 1918, p. 30-37.

————. *Twentieth Census of Living Bison as of January 1, 1934*, New York: American Bison Society, 1934.

————. *A Short History of the American Bison*, New York: American Bison Society, 1934.

————. *The American Bison*, New York: New York Zoological Society, 1938.

Gates, E. "New Meat for the Millions," *American Magazine*, Vol. 67, 1909, pp. 263-270.

Gentry, W. "Buffalo for the Market," *Country Gentleman*, Vol. 81, 1916, p. 1900.

Gillman, W. G. "Traumatic Corditis in a Buffalo Bull," *Journal of the American Veterinary Medical Association*, Vol. 51, 1917, pp. 229-231.

Goodnight, C. "My Experiences with Bison Hybrids," *Journal of Heredity*, Vol. 5, 1914, pp. 197-202.

Graham, M. "Experimental Crossing of Buffalo with Domestic Cattle," *Canadian Veterinary Record*, Vol. 4, 1923, pp. 266-268.

Gray, A. P. *Mammalian Hybrids: A Check-list with Bibliography*, Farnham Royal, Bucks, England: Commonwealth Agricultural Bureaux, 1954.

Griffith, A. S. "Naturally Acquired Tuberculosis in Various Animals. Some Unusual Cases," *Journal of Hygine*, Vol. 36(2), 1936, pp. 156-168.

Grinnell, G. B. "The Last of the Buffalo," *Scribner's Magazine*, Vol. 12(3), 1892, pp. 267-286.

Hadwen, S. "Tuberculosis in the Buffalo," *Journal of the American Veterinary Medical Association*, Vol. 100(778), 1942, pp. 19-22.

Haldane, J. B. S. "Sex Ratio and Unisexual Sterility in Hybrid Animals," *Journal of Genetics*, Vol. 12(2), 1922, pp. 101-109.

Haley, J. E. *Charles Goodnight—Cowman and Plainsman*, New York: Houghton Mifflin Co., 1936.

Halloran, A. F. "Live and Dressed Weights of American Bison," *Journal of Mammalogy*, Vol. 38(1), 1957, p. 139.

Hartung, A. M. "They Tried to Produce a New Kind of Cow," *West Livestock Journal*, Vol. 34(3), 1948, pp. 118-119.

Hawley, S. "New National Bison Herd," *Country Life*, Vol. 25, 1914, p. 136.

Hediger, H. "Zum Verhalten des amerikanischen Bisons bei der Geburt," *Verhandlung der schweizerische naturforschungen Gesellschaft*, Bd. 120, 1940, pp. 174-176.

Hewitt, C. G. "The Coming Back of the Bison," *Natural History*, Vol. 19(6), 1919, pp. 553-565.

Hornaday, W. T. "The Extermination of the American Bison," *Report of the United States National Museum for 1887*, 1890, pp. 367-548.

————. "Bison Comes Back to His Own," *Collier's*, Vol. 44, 1910, p. 20.

Hornecker, M. *Buffalo Hunting on the Texas Plains in 1877*, Geneseo: n.p., 1929.

"How the True Cattalo is Bred," *Scientific American*, Vol. 133, 1925, p. 89.

Hutton, S. "Saving a Royal American Race," *Illustrated World*, Vol. 35, 1921, pp. 245-246.

Innes, J. "Buffalo Hunting," *Canadian Magazine*, Vol. 19, 1902, pp. 9-17.

Iwanoff, E. "Die Fruchtbarkeit der Hybriden des Bos taurus und des Bison americanus," *Biologisches Zentralblatt*, Bd. 31, 1911, pp. 21-24.

————. "Fertilité des hybrides des Bison americanus (female) X Bison europaeus (male)," *C. R. Société Biologie*, [Paris], Vol. 70, 1911, pp. 584-586.

Jackson, A. W. "Present Numbers of Bison in Texas," *Journal of Mammalogy*, Vol. 48(1), 1967, pp. 145-146.

Jellison, W. L.; Stoenmer, H. G.; Dramis, H. J.; and Beardmore, H. F. "An Outbreak of Tick Paralysis in Cattle in Western Montana," *Veterinary Medicine*, Vol. 46, 1951, pp. 163-166.

Johnson, A. "Adding Buffalo Traits to Beef," *Technical World*, Vol. 23, 1915, pp. 359-361.

Johnson, C. W. "Protein as a Factor in the Distribution of the American Bison," *Geographical Review*, Vol. 41(2), 1951, pp. 330-331.

Jones, C. J. *Buffalo Jones' Forty Years of Adventure*, Ed. H. Inman, Topeka, Kansas: Crane and Co., 1899.

————. "My Buffalo Experiments," *Independent*, Vol. 60, 1906, pp. 1351-1355.

————. "Breeding Catalo," *American Breeders' Association Annual Report*, No. 3, 1907, p. 161-165.

Jones, J. J. "Passing of the Buffalo," *Overland Monthly*, Vol. 50, 1907, pp. 156-162.

Jones, T. *The Last of the Buffalo*, Cincinnati: Scenic Souvenirs Publisher [Mimeographed], 1909.

Kitto, F. H. "The Suvival of the American Bison in Canada," *Geographical Journal*, Vol. 63(5), 1924, pp. 431-438.

Kohls, G. M.; and Kramis, N. J. "Tick Paralysis in the American Buffalo, Bison bison (Linn.)," *Northwest Scientist*, Vol. 26(2), 1952, pp. 61-64.

Krasinska, M. "An Immobilizing Cage for Bisons and Hybrids of Bison and Cattle," *Acta Theriologica*, Vol. 12(19/35), 1967, pp. 477-479.

Lapage, G. *Mönnig's Veterinary Helminthology and Entomology*, 5th ed., London: Bailliere, Tindall and Cox, 1962.

Larson, F. "Role of the Bison in Maintaining the Short Grass Plains," *Ecology*, Vol. 21, 1940, pp. 113-121.

"Last Herds," *Harpers' Weekly*, Vol. 56, 1912, p. 17.

Lawson, J. K. *Lawson's History of North Carolina*, New York: Facsimile, Ronald, 1714.

Levie, A. *The Meat Handbook*, Westport, Conn., Avi Publishing Co., 1963.

Lillie, G. W. "Restoring the Bison to the Western Plains," *Cosmopolitan*, Vol. 39, 1905, pp. 651-654.

Locker, B. "Parasites of Bison in Northwestern U.S.A.," *Journal of Parasitology*, Vol. 39(1), 1953, pp. 58-59.

Logan, V. S.; and Sylvestre, P. E. *Hybridization of Domestic Beef Cattle and Buffalo, A Progress Statement, 1950*, Ottawa: Department of Agriculture, Canada, 1950.

McCreight, M. I. *Buffalo Bones Days*, Sykesville: Nupp Printing Co., 1939.

McLaren, A. "A Texas Buffalo Herd," *Outdoor Life*, Vol. 26, 1910, pp. 375-378.

McNary, D. C. "Anthrax in American Bison," *Journal of the American Veterinary Medical Association*, Vol. 112(854), 1948, p. 378.

Malin, J. C. "Soil, Animal, and Plant Relations of the Grasslands," Historically Reconsidered," *Scientific American*, Vol. 76, 1953, pp. 208-209; 220.

Matisko, S. "Cattalo," *Pennsylvania State Farmer*, Vol. 22, 1928, pp. 11, 15.

Mayer, F. H. *The Buffalo Harvest*, Denver: Sage Books, 1958.

"Meat from the Catalo," *Literary Digest*, Vol. 50, 1915, pp. 1212-1213.

Menominee Herald-Leader. " 'Jumbo' Buffalo to Be Part of Herd," *The Herald-Leader*, (16 July), 1970, p. 3.

Merriam, C. "The Buffalo in Northeastern California," *Journal of Mammalogy*, Vol. 7(3), 1926, pp. 211-214.

Merriman, R. O. "The Bison and the Fur Trade," *Queen's Quarterly*, n.v.: (July-September), 1926, pp. 78-96.

Middleton, P. H. "Last Effort to Save the Bison," *Technical World*, Vol. 17, 1912, pp. 519-520.

Miller, W. J. and Stone, W. H. "Blood Typing Erythrocytes of Bison with Reagents for Antigenic Factors of Cattle," *Genetics*, Vol. 40, 1955, p. 586.

Mitchell, H. H. "The Minimum Protein Requirements of Cattle," *Bulletin of the National Research Council, No. 67*, 1929.

Montagnes, J. "Cattalo, the New Quadruped," *Countryman*, Vol. 34, 1946, p. 285.

————. "Add Bison to Cattle and You Have the Cattalo," *National Livestock Producer*, Vol. 25(6), 1947, p. 16.

Moore, C. R. "The Biology of the Testis," In: *Sex and Internal Secretions*, Ed. E. Allen, n.p.: The William and Wilkins Co., 1932.

Moore, S. "West Relived at Bison Run," *The Spokesman-Review*, (2 November), 1969, p. 14e.

National Academy of Sciences and National Research Council. *Nutrient Requirements of Domestic Animals: Report No. IV, Nutrient Requirements of Beef Cattle*, revised edition, Publication No. 1137, Washington, D.C., 1963.

Neal, B. *Last of the Thundering Herd*, New York: McLeod, 1933.

Nelson, J. "How Practical are Cattalo?" *American Feed and Grain Dealer*, Vol. 30(10), 1946, pp. 8-9; 27; 42.

Niedberding, V. "Buffalo Ranch," *Soil Conservation*, Vol. 25, 1952, pp. 44-45.

Novakowski, N. S. "Parasites and Diseases of Bison in Canada; Anthrax epizoatic in the Northwest Territories: with Discussion," *North American Wildlife Conference, Transactions*, Vol. 1963, 1963, pp. 233-239.

_____. "Cemental Deposition as an Age Criterion in Bison, and the Relation of Incisor Wear, Eye Lens Weight, and Dressed Bison Carcass Weight to Age," *Canadian Journal of Zoology*, Vol. 43(1), 1965, pp. 173-178.

Owen, R. D., *et. al.* "Studies in Blood Groups in the American Bison (Buffalo)," *Evolution*, Vol. 12(1), 1958, pp. 102-110.

Paine, B. H. *Pioneers, Indians, and Buffaloes* [sic], Curtis: Curtis Enterprises, 1935.

Palmer, L. J. "Food Requirements of Some Alaskan Game Animals," *Journal of Mammalogy*, Vol. 25(1), 1944, pp. 49-54.

"Passing of the Bison," *Overland Monthly*, Vol. 63, 1914, pp. 442-448.

"Passing of the Buffalo," *Overland Monthly*, Vol. 65, 1915, pp. 437-441.

Perry, E. L. "Remembering the Buffalo," *American Forests*, Vol. 32, 1926, pp. 600-602.

Peters, H. F. "A Feedlot Study of Bison, Cattalo and Hereford Calves," *Canadian Journal of Animal Science*, Vol. 38, 1958, pp. 87-90.

_____. *Experience with Yak Crosses in Canada, Adapted from Reports of the Wainwright Experiment on Hybridization of Domestic Cattle, American bison, and Yak*, Ottawa: Canadian Department of Agriculture [mimeograph], 1968.

_____; and Newbound, K. B. "Intra-testicular Temperature and Fertility of Bison, Cattalo, and Hereford Yearling Bulls," *Canadian Journal of Animal Science*, Vol. 37, 1957, pp. 14-20.

_____; and Slen, S. B. "Hair Coat Characteristics of Bison, Domestic X Domestic Hybrids, Cattalo, and Certain Breeds of Beef Cattle," *Canadian Journal of Animal Science*, Vol. 44, 1964, pp. 48-57.

_____; _____. "Range Calf Production of Cattle X Bison, Cattalo, and Hereford Cows," *Canadian Journal of Animal Science*, Vol. 46, 1966, pp. 157-164.

Phillips, R. W. "Bovine Hybrids," *Cattleman*, Vol. 33(3), 1946, pp. 13-16; 52.

Pinkerton, J. *A General Collection of the Best and Most Interesting Voyages and Travels in All Parts of the World*, 17 vols., London: Longman, Hurst, Rees, Orme, and Brown, 1812.

Purchas, S. *Hakluytus Posthumus or Purchas His Pilgrimes* [sic], 20 vols., Glasgow: James MacLehose and Sons, 1906.

Raudabush, R. L. "Arthropod and Helminth Parasites of the American Bison," *Journal of Parasitology*, Vol. 22, 1936, pp. 517-518.

"Return of the Buffalo," *Nor'-west Farmer*, Vol. 45, 1926, p. 31.

Roe, F. G. *The North American Buffalo: A Critical Study of the Species in its Wild State*, Toronto: University of Toronto Press, 1970.

Ross, A. *Red River Settlement*, London: Smith, Elder, and Co., 1856.

Rostlund, E. "The Geographic Range of the Historic Bison in the Southeast," *Annals of the Association of American Geographers*, Vol. 50(4), 1960, pp. 395-407.

Rush, W. M. "Bang's Disease in the Yellowstone National Park Buffalo and Elk Herds," *Journal of Mammalogy*, Vol. 13(4), 1932, pp. 371-372.

Sanders, H. F. "National Bison Park," *Overland Monthly*, Vol. 53, 1909, pp. 116-119.

Sandoz, M. *The Buffalo Hunters*, New York: Hastings House, 1954.

Schrauder, E. A. "Where the Buffalo Roam; Trexler-Leigh County Game Preserve, Pa.," *American Forests*, Vol. 67, 1961, p. 5.

Seelye-Miller, R. "Passing and the Comeback of the Buffalo," *Rural New York*, Vol. 85, 1926, p. 164.

Seton, E. T. *Lives of Game Animals*, 4 vols., New York: Doubleday, Page and Co., 1927.

Shaw, D. H.; and Patel, J. R. "Species Differences between the American Bison and Domestic Cattle Determined by Heteroimmune Hemolysins," *American Zoologist*, Vol. 1(3), 1961, pp. 387-388.

———; and ———. "Demonstration of Antigenic Difference Between American Bison and Domestic Cattle," *Nature*, Vol. 196(4853), 1962, pp. 498-499.

Sheng, T. S. "Virus encephalomyelitis in Buffaloes [sic]," *Science*, Vol. 103, 1946, p. 344.

Shoemaker, H. W. *Pennsylvania Bison Hunt*, Middleburg: Middleburg Post Press, 1915.

Simpson, Q. I. "Rejuvenation by Hybridization," *American Breeders' Association*, Vol. 3, 1907, pp. 76-81.

Slaughter, B. "Vanquished Lord," *Texas Game and Fish*, Vol. 18(1), 1960, pp. 24-25.

Smoliak, S.; and Peters, H. F. "Climatic Effects on Foraging Performance of Beef Cows on Winter Range," *Canadian Journal of Animal Science*, Vol. 35, 1955, pp. 213-216.

"Some Buffalo Encounters," *Literary Digest*, Vol. 78, 1923, pp. 62-64.

Soper, J. D. "History, Range and Home Life of the Northern Bison," *Ecological Monographs*, Vol. 11, 1941, pp. 347-412.

Starzynski, W. "Use of the Palmer Gun to Immobilize European Bison," *Acta Theriologica*, Vol. 12(19/35), 1967, pp. 471-472.

Stormont, C. "A Further Comparison of Bison and Cattle Tranferrins," In: *48th Annual Meeting of the Federation of American Societies for Experimental Biology, Proceedings*, Vol. 23 (2, part 1), 1964, p. 557.

————; Miller, W. J.; and Suzuki, Y. "Blood Groups and Taxonomic Status of American Buffalo and Domestic Cattle, *Evolution*, Vol. 15, 1961, pp. 196-208.

Stuckenschneider, H. "Will the Buffalo Roam . . . Again?" *Record Stockman*, Vol. 80, 1969, pp. 148-149.

Surface, B. "The Buffalo is Back!" *Readers' Digest*, Vol. 90(541), 196?, pp. 189-194.

Sylvestre, P. E.; Logan, V. S.; and Muir, G. W. "Hybridization of Domestic Cattle and the Bison," *Canadian Department of Agriculture Report*, 1948.

Szaniawski, A. "Comparison of Digestibility of Foodstuffs with Different Protein Ratios for Calves of Domestic Cattle and of Bison," *Acta Theriologica*, Vol. 3(13), 1960, pp. 318-319.

Tait, W. M. "New Source of Wool Supply in Canada, a Buffalo," *Farmers' Advocate*, Vol. 55, 1920, p. 1568.

Thompson, A. W. "Last of the Buffalo in Texas," *Cattleman*, Vol. 14(11), 1930, pp. 29-31.

Tunniclif, E. A.; and Marsh, H. "Bang's Disease in Bison and Elk in the Yellowstone National Park and on the National Bison Range," *Journal of the American Veterinary Medical Association*, Vol. 86, 1935, pp. 745-752.

Turner, J. P. "The Story of the Buffalo," *Geographical Magazine*, Vol. 3(4), 1936, pp. 221-234.

United States Congress, The Senate. *To Establish a Permanent National Bison Range: A Report*, Report No. 467, 1908.

"Want a Buffaloburger?" *Farm Quarterly*, Vol. 7, 1952, pp. 50-51.

Warren, E. R. "A Silk Buffalo Robe," *Journal of Mammalogy*, Vol. 2(3), 1921, pp. 173-174.

Wheeler, D. "Oh, They Have a Home Where the Catalo Roam," *The Billings Gazette Sunday Magazine*, (1 December), 1968, p. 15.

Whitney, C. "Working to Save the Bison," *Outing*, Vol. 50, 1907, pp. 102-106.

Widmer, J. *Practical Beef Production*, New York: Scribner's, 1946.

Wilber, C. G.; and Gorski, T. W. "The Lipids of Bison bison," *Journal of Mammalogy*, Vol. 36(2), 1955, pp. 305-308.

Williamson, G. Y. "Story of the American Buffalo," *Science Digest*, Vol. 20, 1946, pp. 57-61.

Wilson, L. C. "Catalo Breeding," *Producer*, Vol. 12(1), 1930, p. 8.

Winsor, J., Ed. *Narrative and Critical History of America*, 8 vols., Boston: Houghton Mifflin, 1884-89.

Worley, D. E. "Chemotherapeutic Studies of Gastrointestinal Parasites of Beef Cattle and Bison in Kansas," *American Journal of Veterinary Research*, Vol. 21(82), 1960, pp. 416-421.

————; and Hansen, M. F. "Chemotherapeutic Studies of Gastrointestinal Parasites of Beef Cattle and Bison in Kansas," *Journal of the American Veterinary Medical Association*, Vol. 137, 1960, p. 377.

INDEX

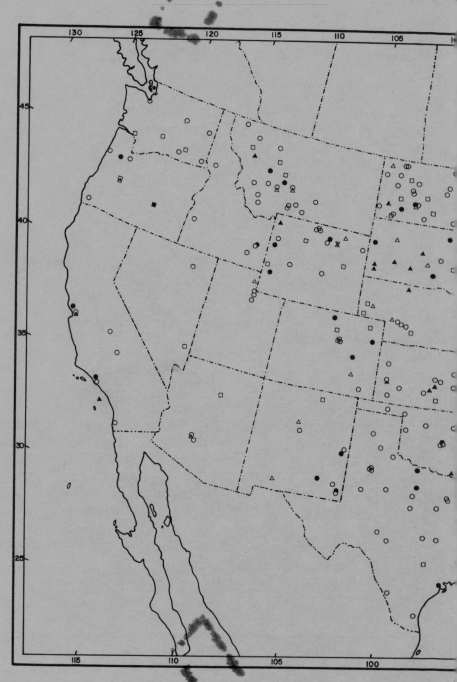

Distribution of Buff